THE THIRTIES

AMERICA and the GREAT DEPRESSION

THE THIRTIES

AMERICA and the GREAT DEPRESSION

FON W. BOARDMAN, JR.

New York
HENRY Z. WALCK, INC.
1967

LIBRARY OF CONGRESS CATALOG CARD NUMBER: 67-19921
PRINTED IN THE UNITED STATES OF AMERICA

For
Rhea Boardman Underwood

Contents

1 *Prosperity and Herbert Hoover*

On March 4, 1929, Herbert Clark Hoover was inaugurated as the thirty-first President of the United States, a peaceful, prosperous nation, well pleased with itself and with its choice for the nation's highest elective office.

Hoover was perfectly qualified to represent the American ideal of the time. Born in rural Iowa in 1874, he had been a campus leader at Stanford University, from which he graduated in 1895. His qualities both as a mining engineer and as an executive were quickly recognized: the firm he worked for sent him to Australia and to China; when he was twenty-five years old he was already making $20,000 a year (the equivalent of four or five times that amount in terms of today's living costs and taxes); and two years later he was a junior partner of one of the world's leading engineering firms, with headquarters in London.

The start of World War I in Europe in the summer of 1914 brought Hoover into public life for the first time and gave play to two aspects of his background and personality: his Quaker upbringing and his organizational ability. As chairman of the American Relief Commission he arranged means for getting 150,000 stranded Americans home from Europe. From 1915 to 1919, as chairman of the Commission for Relief in Belgium, he successfully persevered in the difficult and delicate task of arranging for food and clothing for

Belgian civilians whose country had been overrun by the Germans. It was not surprising that, when the United States entered the war, Herbert Hoover became Food Administrator and his name a household word: "Don't put so much sugar on your cereal or Mr. Hoover will get you."

Next, he was quite naturally the leading figure in American relief work in Europe after the war. He entered political life at the Cabinet level and served as Secretary of Commerce from 1921 to 1929 under Presidents Harding and Coolidge. Here again his talents as a planner and organizer came into play. He held conferences on such problems as unemployment and the allocation of radio broadcasting wave lengths; he encouraged businessmen to form trade associations and to agree on fair rules of competition; he supported public engineering projects for irrigation and power facilities. He believed the Federal government should do nothing to regulate or control business or labor but should encourage all private efforts that would increase business activity and prosperity.

Since American economic life prospered greatly during these years and since Hoover was such a contrast of honesty and efficiency compared with most of his high-level colleagues of the time, he almost inevitably became the most talked-of prospect for the Republican nomination for the presidency in 1928. All that kept him from being a much loved, as well as a much admired, public figure was his personality. With his plain, always unsmiling face set firmly over a high stiff collar, he seemed completely humorless—a planning and thinking machine rather than a human being.

In the summer of 1928 he received the Republican nomination almost without opposition. In accepting the nomination at ceremonies in August, he said: "We in America today are nearer to the final triumph over poverty than ever before in the history of any land. The poorhouse is vanishing from among us. We have not yet reached the goal, but, given a chance to go forward with the policies of the last eight years, we shall soon with the help of God be in sight of the day when poverty will be banished from this nation." Hoover sincerely believed this and, on the basis of his interpretation of the economic situation, he did not see how his vision could fail to come true.

Hoover's opponent was Alfred E. Smith, who won the Democratic nomination on the first ballot after being praised as "the Happy Warrior" by Franklin D. Roosevelt. There could have been no sharper contrast in public life than that between Smith and Hoover. Smith, who had an excellent record as governor of New York State, was a New York City Irish Catholic—the first city-bred candidate and the first Catholic contender for the presidency the nation had had. In addition, Smith stood plainly and frankly for repeal of the prohibition amendment. Smith's Catholicism hurt him in rural areas, his "wetness" hurt him in the South and the West, but for the first time the people of the urban areas of the North and East had a spokesman of their own. More than ever before, radio played a key part in the campaign and carried the voices of the candidates to anyone who cared to listen. Smith's cause was hurt by his rasping voice and his "New York accent." He said "raddio" for "radio." The voters chose Hoover with his staid air of propriety and prosperity. The popular vote was 21,392,000 to 15,016,000 and in the electoral college Hoover received 444 to Smith's 87. Smith carried only eight states and Hoover and the Republicans even won part of the normally Democratic South. In New York State, however, Smith's friend and supporter, Roosevelt, was elected governor by a narrow margin while his running mate lost the state overwhelmingly to Hoover.

And so, in early 1929, Hoover became the chief executive of a nation that recently had been transformed in many ways as a result of its role in World War I. The United States had come out of that war in an entirely different position than when the war began. For one thing, America was now at least as powerful as any nation on earth. Also, the United States suddenly had become a creditor nation. Unfortunately, as time would show, the nation did not want to accept the responsibilities that go with military, political, and financial power. Quite understandably, it wanted to forget about the war and about the quarrels of Europe and Asia. It wanted to enjoy in peace the multitude of goods and gadgets it had discovered its modern, efficient industrial plants could produce in ever greater quantities.

There had been one short depression in 1920–21, but otherwise economic growth had been almost unbroken for nearly a decade. Most of the population of about 123,000,000 was living better than ever. The movement of the American people from rural to urban areas, which had been going on for many years, speeded up in the 1920's. In 1870 about half of all persons gainfully employed worked in agriculture but by 1930 only about one-fifth were farmers. The wages paid in the mammoth automobile factories lured many people from the country and many Negroes from the South to the North. And, as the Doughboys of World War I sang, "How ya gonna keep 'em down on the farm after they've seen Paree?"

Business was king. The nation's idols (except for movie stars) were not military or political figures but businessmen. *Time* magazine's "Man of the Year" in January, 1929, was Walter P. Chrysler, auto manufacturer. Andrew Mellon, Hoover's Secretary of the Treasury, was one of the richest and most powerful industrialists in the country. Under business leadership and unhampered by government controls, the quantity of goods produced by each factory worker had steadily increased, wages were higher, everybody seemed to have more of everything, and even the five-day work week was coming in. At least this was the business point of view, and all but the Socialists and some of the liberals had to agree. Business organizations were getting larger and larger. Only troublemakers, though, saw anything wrong with, or worried overmuch about, the separation of ownership (the possession of shares in a business or industrial corporation) and management (the men who held the executive positions and ran the business pretty much as they saw fit). The large corporation, not the business owned and managed by one or two men, was now the most important form of organization.

And yet, if one looks closely and especially when one has the advantage of hindsight, all was not well even as Hoover took the oath of office. Business was making more money than ever, but too large a proportion of it went into profits, partly paid out in dividends to the stockholders, and too little into wage increases for the workmen. Wages went up, but not in proper relation to profits and productivity. Prices did not go down as the cost of production decreased. Foreign trade seemed to boom but it was not in a healthy balance. Americans were investing large sums of money abroad, some of it in the bonds of unstable governments. At the same time, our high tariffs, our high prices, and the vast sums already owed us for money we had loaned to our allies during the war made it impossible for the rest of the world to buy from us in anything like the amounts we were sending abroad—unless they bought our goods with the very money we were lending them.

The general prosperity also obscured weak points in the condition of the laboring man. While, on the whole, no nation's blue-collar workers had ever lived as well, they were actually losing ground in relation to business and the well-to-do class. Residential and industrial building, the growth of the electric utility companies, and especially the continued expansion of the automobile industry created many jobs. On the other hand, there was much technological unemployment all through the 1920's, especially in coal mining, railroads, and the textile industry. Organized labor, while not prevented by law from carrying on its activities, was still rather generally looked upon as slightly un-American, except perhaps for some of the more highly skilled crafts. Business did its best to prevent unionization of industry. It was ably assisted by the complacency and incompetence of those who controlled the organized labor movement—the American Federation of Labor. Union membership had reached a peak of just over 5,000,000 in 1920 but then fell all during the decade. By 1929 there were not quite 3,500,000 members, or only about 10 per cent of the non-agricultural work force. In addition to employer opposition and the lethargy of union leadership, the very fact of general prosperity and no great increase in the cost of living gave the workingman a sense of well-being he was reluctant to jeopardize by joining a union and, perhaps, having to march on a picket line.

In one of the largest and most basic areas of American economic life—agriculture—no one disputed the fact that something was wrong, but there was great difference of opinion as to what, if anything, should be done about it. During the war and early postwar years—from 1915 to 1920—American agriculture prospered because of the worldwide, war-inspired demand for its products. In the 1920's, though, the foreign markets shrank as other nations tried to supply their own needs and as new farm lands were opened in such countries as Canada and Australia. Food consumption at home did not increase for several reasons. There was a slowing down in the rate at which the population was growing and there were changes in eating habits. Synthetic fibers began to replace cotton and wool. Even the use of more and better machines on the farms helped depress the prices the farmer received because fewer farmers could produce more food than ever. Tenant farmers and sharecroppers suffered most of all. In 1919 the nation's farmers had had a total income of $15,000,000,000, but by 1929 this was down to $12,000,000,000 while the prices of the goods the farmers had to buy continued to go up.

In fact, agriculture was the one field in which President Hoover approved action by the Federal government early in his term of office. In June, 1929, the Federal Farm Board was established by law to try to hold steady the prices of farm products by buying up surpluses on the open market. However, since the farmers, a very individualistic lot, were under no compulsion to hold down their production, they grew bigger crops than ever in the hope of profiting from the government purchasing program. The Federal Farm Board eventually had to sell its holdings at a loss of about $200,000,000.

The uneven way in which the prosperity Hoover inherited was spread among the nation's families was another sign that all was not well. Only 8.2 per cent of the country's families had incomes of $5,000 or more a year, but they received 42 per cent—nearly half—of the total income of all families. On the other hand, 59.5 per cent of the families received $2,000 or less a year and they got only 23.7 per cent of the total. Economists would later point to this as a cause of the Great Depression: the great mass of the workers did not get in wages enough money to buy the things they produced, while a smaller group, taking in more money than they could spend, saved more money than was needed for investment in new machinery and new enterprises.

In those days, too, there were few of the social welfare benefits that we take for granted today. Unemployment insurance was virtually unknown, as were medical and hospital insurance plans. There was no social security system to provide even a minimum income in old age. At the same time, the proportion of older people in the population was increasing and by 1929 there were more than 6,000,000 persons aged sixty-five or over. Urban life and modern machinery made it harder than in earlier times for older people to hold a job and to earn a living.

Most, if not all, Americans were too busy with other and more exciting matters in 1929 to examine closely any such cracks in prosperity's façade. If they read any business news at all, it was probably a quick glance to see how much the stock market had gone up the day before. The excitement and the pleasures of city life were becoming the American ideal, rather than the highly praised healthful serenity of the countryside. A generation earlier more than half the people lived in rural areas; now more than half were town and city dwellers. The city of Los Angeles, with a little more than 300,000 citizens in 1910, now had more than a million. Washington, D.C., with somewhat fewer than 200,000 inhabitants in 1890, was approaching the half-million mark.

Along with this constantly increasing urbanization of the nation, the greatest change in the way Americans lived resulted from the enormous increase in the number of automobiles and trucks in use. In 1910 there were only 458,000 autos in the whole United States and by the end of World War I only 9,000,000, but by 1929 there were more than 26,000,000. In 1929 the nation's auto factories turned out almost 5,500,000 units, a figure that would not be reached again for nearly a decade. In 1928, after having produced 15,000,000 of his Model T cars, Henry Ford brought out his Model A and the American people got more excited about it than about the presidential election. Such cars, incidentally, cost only a few hundred dollars. While Ford is still one of the best-known names among cars, a good many others have disappeared: Franklin, Pierce-Arrow, Auburn, Locomobile, for example. The first trailer was produced in 1929, traffic signals were being erected, most autos were now sedans rather than open touring cars, and buses were starting to replace trolley cars. The death toll from motor vehicle accidents was also on the rise, the yearly total already being more than 30,000.

As many statistics showed, Americans did not buy their autos just to admire them. No nation in history had been half as mobile and this was reflected most of all in the growth of a whole new retail industry—the service station. The town dweller could picnic in the country whenever he wanted to, spelling, incidentally, the doom of the once popular interurban trolley. The farmer, in spite of thousands of miles of dirt roads not yet turned into concrete and asphalt, could visit the big city, and young people could get away from the confines of the front parlor and parental supervision. This was a revolution in social life as well as transportation.

New ways of doing things were being introduced in other areas. It was now smart to eat plenty of food containing vitamins. This proved a boon to the citrus-fruit growers, the truck gardeners, and the dairy farmers. And with fewer people performing heavy physical labor, there was less demand for cereals, potatoes, and meat. The first supermarkets were appearing in Los Angeles where there were twenty-five of them in 1929. Shoppers were increasingly buying food and other products in chain store branches. Between 1918 and 1929 chain store units increased from 29,000 to 160,000, and the number of A&P stores was already in five figures. When it came to purchasing more expensive items, such as autos and refrigerators, installment buying was just becoming part of the American way of life.

Along with the automobile, radio broadcasting was the most noticeable influence in changing the way people spent their leisure time in the 1920's. From one broadcasting station in 1920, the industry by 1929 had already grown to hundreds of stations, many of them affiliated with the networks of the National Broadcasting Company and the Columbia Broadcasting System. In 1929 radio sets still cost over $100 but there were already 12,000,000 of them around the United States. Many of them still operated on batteries and had earphones instead of speakers. The nation spent $852,000,000 that year on sets and parts. Within a decade an entirely new industry had become an important support of business prosperity. It was in 1929 also that "Amos 'n' Andy" became a network program and the most popular show radio ever produced. The two comedians who wrote it and played all the parts, Freeman Gosden and Charles Correll, almost brought the life of the nation to a standstill each time they went on the air. It was also fun to stay up late at night to try to bring in distant stations. Turning the dial in New York State, you might be lucky enough to pick up Davenport, Iowa.

Movies were more popular than ever because, beginning in 1927, they had become talkies. Producers and actors were still feeling their way around in this new invention in 1929, and such popular stars as Mary Pickford and Joan Crawford made their first talkies. Some popular movies of the year were *Disraeli,* with George Arliss; *What Price Glory; The Love Parade,* with Maurice Chevalier and Jeanette MacDonald; *The Broadway Melody,* one of the first of a crop of glossy, flashy musicals; and the first *Silly Symphony.*

The Jazz Age was nearly over even though the flappers and their escorts in wide-bottomed trousers didn't know it yet. Women's skirts were almost up to the knee, but they would soon go down and would not rise as high again for a decade.

There was excitement for everyone, depending on what one was interested in. The Museum of Modern Art in New York City was founded in 1929, and Richard E. Byrd, soon to be a rear admiral for his feat, with Bernt Balchen flew over the South Pole in an airplane. The German dirigible, the *Graf Zeppelin,* flew around the world, but there was not yet regular transcontinental air service in the United States. A traveler could, by a new arrangement, get from New York to the West Coast in the record time of forty-eight hours by riding trains at night and planes during the day. For the sports-minded there was Babe Ruth, the greatest home run slugger baseball has ever seen, and Big Bill Tilden, who won the United States amateur tennis championship for the seventh time. For the book-minded, this was a memorable year, especially for first or early novels: Ernest Hemingway's *A Farewell to Arms;* Thomas Wolfe's *Look Homeward, Angel;* and William Faulkner's *The Sound and the Fury.* In nonfiction, two books that were to have an impact on the world were Robert and Helen Lynd's *Middletown* and Walter Lippmann's *A Preface to Morals.*

The most absorbing subject for many people, however, was prohibition. For nearly ten years now it had been illegal—and theoretically impossible—to buy a glass of beer, a cocktail, or a bottle of liquor to take home. The Eighteenth Amendment to the Constitution of the United States and the Volstead Act had said so. In practice, though, the situation was considerably different. Liquor was being smuggled into the country by land and by sea. Many people were making their own "home brew" or "bathtub gin." In every city and most small towns the speak-easy and the bootlegger had become well-established institutions. If one knew the proprietor or the password, a knock on the door would admit one to what formerly had been known as a saloon and what after prohibition ended would be more delicately known as a tavern. The wets said prohibition was both an infringement of individual rights and unenforceable. The drys had to admit that the country had not stopped drinking the way it was supposed to, but more prohibition agents or more moral persuasion would eventually solve the problem. Only the blindest, however, could deny the increase in crime and racketeering. The most spectacular crime of the year was the "St. Valentine's Day Massacre" in Chicago on February 14 when a group of gangsters mowed down seven members of a rival gang at one time. Hoover soon appointed a commission to study the whole question of law enforcement and crime—a group that became known as the Wickersham Commission, after its chairman George W. Wickersham.

This was America and these were some of the interests and attitudes of the American people in the booming year of 1929 as Mr. and Mrs. Herbert Hoover moved into the White House. Not one American in a thousand would have believed a prophet who foretold within a matter of months the crashing onset of the worst depression the nation has ever known. Anyone could see that this country had discovered the magical formula for perpetual prosperity. Under the wise guidance of the managers of big business and the Republican party (to many the two seemed much the same thing) everyone was certain to get richer every year.

Indeed, it would have been as difficult then to convince anyone of what was going to happen as it is today to explain to the children and grandchildren of those who lived through the ensuing Great Depression of 1929–39 what it was really like. Because of World War II and the rapid march of events of that era and all the troubled years since, the depression seems somehow to be even further in the past than it really is. In some ways, the Great Depression was worse than the war that followed it. There were no marching songs or medals; there was no excitement. In the war, for many, the body died suddenly; in the depression, for many, the spirit died slowly.

Many writers and speakers have confessed their inability to make a new generation understand what the depression felt like. Granville Hicks, a perceptive writer who was active in radical politics and the literary world of the era, recently wrote:

> For a long time now I have found it difficult, when talking to college audiences about the Thirties, to make undergraduates understand what a depression is like. These boys and girls are so completely children of the Age of Affluence that they cannot conceive of joblessness, poverty, and despair on a nation-wide scale. I cite figures and tell them some of the things I saw with my own eyes, but there is nothing in their experience to help them to grasp what I am talking about.

It is, indeed, difficult to explain what life was like in the Great Depression and why, and how it colors even today the thoughts and actions of a generation that still, on the whole, runs the world.

2 The Biggest Stock Market Crash in the World

THE PEACEFUL YEAR OF 1929 turned out to be one of the most unforgettable in American history. Like 1775, 1861, and 1941, it became a dividing line between two eras. Life in America was never the same again. However, unlike those other years, which marked the beginnings of wars, 1929 was deceptively quiet. Instead of guns booming on battlefields, what typified the year and forever gave 1929 its place in history was a mass of business transactions centered in a few offices in New York City. This was the year of "The Great Crash."

By the mid-1920's people all over the United States were talking about "the stock market," or just "the market." They were referring to the New York Stock Exchange, the largest and by far the most influential of the various organized centers for buying and selling shares of stock in hundreds of corporations. In previous generations the stock market had been the preserve of the biggest businessmen and the large-scale speculators. Now that mass production and mass prosperity had arrived, why shouldn't the stock market be opened to the masses also? Bankers and stockbrokers were in favor of this because they benefited by lending money and by taking commissions on stocks they bought and sold for their customers.

With the generally excellent business conditions of the 1920's, stocks, quite naturally and properly, had been rising steadily in value. The profits of corporations were increasing and dividends were growing larger. Investment in common stocks was a sound way, so it seemed, to increase both one's income and the value of one's invested capital. Then, early in 1928, as most experts now agree, the basic nature of activities on the stock exchange changed. Stocks were no longer being bought and sold on the basis of their current and prospective value in strict relation to the condition of the company whose assets were represented by its stock. Instead, speculation became dominant. Stocks were bought and sold because it was assumed by everyone that they were going to go up and up and that, no matter how much one paid, in a few days someone else would be willing to pay even more.

The Big Bull Market began in March, 1928. Thereafter, stock prices kept going up and more and more individuals, most of whom did not understand what it was all about, began dabbling in the buying and selling of stocks. At the same time, the professional traders found it more than ever to their advantage as insiders to manipulate stock prices. Hoover's election was followed in November by a new boom in prices and in the number of shares bought and sold. On November 16, 1928, 6,641,250 shares changed hands, up to then the largest single day's business in the history of the New York Stock Exchange. Stock prices fell sharply in December, but the year ended with the *New York Times* average of industrial stocks showing a gain for the twelve months of 86 points. During the year, the Radio Corporation of America (RCA) went up to 420 from 85 even though it had never paid a dividend. Du Pont was 525, up from 310.

By this time the stock market was front-page news. Even people who were not speculating followed the market prices and averages in the same American spirit that caused thousands to be able to tell you offhand any time during the baseball season what the batting average of their favorite star was. New York brokerage houses opened offices in small country towns like Storm Lake, Iowa, and Wellsville, New York.

It is true that only about one and a half million people—not much more than 1 per cent of the population—were actively engaged in buying and selling stocks and not all of them just for the purpose of making a quick profit. The conditions under which the market was operating were, however, such that they affected the whole country more than this figure indicates. For one thing, much of the buying was being done "on margin," which meant with borrowed money. It was a very simple system and profitable for all concerned—as long as it worked. Banks loaned money to stockbrokers who in turn loaned it to would-be stock purchasers who could not, or did not wish to, pay cash for the stocks they bought. The stocks in turn were put up as collateral for the loans. If a person did not pay back the loan when due (actually, this kind of loan was payable on demand), the broker or bank simply sold the securities and kept as much of the proceeds as was needed to recover the money. There were no laws then controlling the amount of cash a person had to put up when buying stock.

The process was tempting to banks because the interest rates they could charge were much higher than on most other loans. During the last week of 1928 the rate on brokers' loans reached 12 per cent. Money poured in from other countries to be loaned out at these profitable rates. Other businesses, such as oil companies, found it more profitable to lend their available money for stock speculation purposes than to invest it in producing more of their companies' goods. At the end of 1927 brokers' loans totaled about $3,500,000,000; by the end of 1928 the amount was up to $5,700,000,000.

The formation and promotion of investment trusts and holding companies also fed the boom by providing many thousands more shares of stock for the public to buy and sell without actually creating any new business or even any assets. Such activities, and many others that were carried on in the late 1920's, were possible because there were then almost no laws governing the manner in which banks, brokers, and corporations operated.

The investment trusts were much like the mutual funds of today, except there were no protective rules concerning how they were formed or managed. An investment trust existed to buy the stocks of other companies. In 1928, 186 of them were launched and in 1929, 265 new ones appeared. It was estimated that $3,000,000,000 worth of trust stock was sold. Trusts were formed by banks, by brokerage houses, and before long investment trusts were spawning new trusts. The firms and individuals sponsoring the trusts received large and early benefits. Part of the scheme provided for them to be paid a regular fee for managing the trust; and at the start those on the inside were able to buy the new shares at prices that were, in the enthusiasm of the times, sure to go up in a few days. In one such deal, involving the irreproachable J. P. Morgan and Company, the insiders were able to make a profit of $14 a share in less than two weeks. Goldman, Sachs and Company, an investment banking and brokerage firm, was a shining example of what could be done without saturating the demand of the innocent investors for more stocks. In less than a year it sponsored the Goldman Sachs Trading Corporation, the Shenandoah Corporation, the Blue Ridge Corporation, and had the first of these trusts buy a West Coast trust that in turn had bought some other smaller trusts. In less than a month, at one point, Goldman, Sachs issued more than $250,000,000 worth of securities. Anyone could issue as many shares of stock as the public was willing to buy. No one had to account to the man who invested his few hundred dollars of savings with the geniuses of Wall Street.

The holding company was another device for acquiring wealth and industrial power at little cost to the man who did the manipulating. The holding companies in the 1920's operated mostly in the public utilities field, especially electric power companies, for in the age of electricity the nation every year consumed more power than before. The organizers of a holding company sold stock to the public but they always retained enough, or enough of the stock that had voting rights, to control the corporation. With funds secured from the public, the holding company bought sufficient stock to get control of a number of the companies that created and sold electric power (or, in some cases, operated railroads). If it seemed desirable, in order to produce more insiders' profits, another holding company would be formed to buy up control of one or more holding companies that already existed. This pyramiding process contributed nothing to the efficiency of electric power production, and while most states regulated the power producers, they had no control over the holding companies. By the time of the depression ten holding-company groups controlled 72 per cent of the country's electric power capacity. Among these were such firms as the Niagara Hudson Company and the Commonwealth and Southern Corporation. As with the investment trusts and stocks in general, the fever for making profits by buying and selling stock pushed the prices of holding-company stocks far beyond their true worth.

September 3, 1929, was a historic day on the New York Stock Exchange. On that day stocks reached an all-time high. RCA was now selling at 505—and still had never paid a dividend. United States Steel reached 262; American Telephone and Telegraph, 304; General Electric, 396. Yet this was the day the Big Bull Market of the 1920's ended. Two days later there was a sharp drop in prices. U.S. Steel went down to 246 and the volume of trading increased, indicating that some people were getting out of the market. Economist Roger Babson was blamed by Wall Street because he had said: "Sooner or later a crash is coming, and it may be terrific." The brokers and bankers much preferred another economist, Irving

Fisher, who decided: "There may be a recession in stock prices, but not anything in the nature of a crash."

Stock prices slowly weakened until late October. Then, on Black Thursday, October 24, panic struck the stock market. At the start of the day's trading the only unusual sign was the large volume of business. (Before the day was over a new record of 12,894,650 shares would be set.) Next, prices began to fall, and the ticker that told brokers and their customers what stocks were selling for fell farther and farther behind. By 11:30 A.M. panic reigned. There was confusion on the floor of the Exchange and a crowd began to gather outside in the street. An hour later officials closed the visitors' gallery. One of the visitors that day was Winston Churchill, who until recently had been the British Chancellor of the Exchequer.

All kinds of rumors began to spread, some of them concerning the number of big speculators who, it was mistakenly alleged, had already committed suicide. Then it was learned that the leading bankers were meeting in the offices of J. P. Morgan and Company, with Thomas W. Lamont as host. Among those present were Charles E. Mitchell, chairman of the board of the National City Bank, and Albert H. Wiggin, chairman of the Chase National Bank. Everyone expected they would save the day, and they did decide to try to stay the panic. When the meeting ended, Mr. Lamont told reporters, in one of the world's greatest understatements: "There has been a little distress selling on the Stock Exchange." The bankers agreed to act by buying stocks to show their confidence. They sent Richard Whitney, vice president of the Exchange, to the floor where, confident and unruffled, he bid 205 for U.S. Steel shares, several points higher than anyone else was bidding at that time. He placed the same kinds of orders for some other stocks. The panic was over for the day and prices went up. It was after seven that evening before the lagging ticker finished tapping out the last transaction and clerks worked most of the night trying to catch up with the paper work.

On the following Monday prices plunged downward again and this time the bankers made no attempt to reverse the trend. They met but decided to do nothing more. The next morning, Tuesday, October 29, ushered in the most catastrophic day ever known to the New York Stock Exchange. Enormous blocks of stock were thrown on the market. By the end of the day another new record of 16,410,030 shares traded had been set, a record that still stands. The ticker was two and a half hours behind and again clerks worked all night in the brokerage houses. Thousands of investors—speculators, if you prefer—were wiped out, and the big operator as well as the little man saw himself ruined.

The next day *The New York Times* reported: "Efforts to estimate yesterday's market losses in dollars are futile. . . . However, it was estimated that 880 issues, on the New York Stock Exchange, lost between $8,000,000,000 and $9,000,000,000. . . . The crowds about the ticker tape, like friends around the bedside of a stricken friend, reflected in their faces the story the tape was telling. There were no smiles. There were no tears either. Just the camaraderie of fellow-sufferers. Everybody wanted to tell his neighbor how much he had lost. Nobody wanted to listen. It was too repetitious a tale. . . ." *Variety,* the show business magazine, summed it up in a headline: "Wall Street Lays an Egg."

On that terrible day, AT&T was down 28 points and so was General Electric. Westinghouse, which had stood at 286 in early September, opened at 131 and dropped to 100. Some of the investment trusts just about disappeared. Goldman Sachs Trading Corporation lost almost half its value, dropping from 65 to 35. Nor was the end in sight, even though there were some short-lived rallies on other days. The market reached its lowest point on November 13, and in the course of the autumn stocks lost about $30,000,000,000 of value. Even so, those involved did not yet know that things were going to get worse before they got better. The *Times* average of industrial stocks was down to 224 in November, 1929, but by July, 1932, it would hit 58. In three years General Motors was to go down from 73 to 8 and U.S. Steel from 262 to 22. In all of 1929, 1,124,800,000 shares were traded on the New York Stock Exchange.

Shortly after the crash, the fabulously wealthy John D. Rockefeller, then ninety years old, announced: "Believing that fundamental conditions of the country are sound . . . my son and I have for some days been purchasing sound common stocks." A little later the comedian Eddie Cantor remarked: "Sure, who else had any money left?"

Some of those who had been heroes of the Big Bull Market turned out in the course of the next few years to have been, at the least, unethical and, at best, as mistaken about the nature of prosperity as the most innocent and ignorant of smalltime speculators. Among them were two of the most powerful bankers of the day, the already mentioned Charles E. Mitchell of the National City Bank and Albert H. Wiggin of the Chase National Bank.

Mitchell ran into several problems. In 1928 his salary and share of profits was $1,316,634. It was even greater in 1929. Much of this, it might be noted, came from the profits of a subsidiary of the bank that was set up solely to market securities, something the bank itself could not do. At this time, too, some of his own stock in the bank was pledged to J. P. Morgan and Company for a loan in connection with a merger deal that fell through because of the stock market crash. Nevertheless, Mitchell sold this stock—18,300 shares—to his wife at a lower price than he had paid for it and thus established a loss of nearly $3,000,000 for tax purposes. As a result he owed no income tax for 1929 in spite of his princely income. Later he admitted at a Senate hearing that he had carried out this transaction for tax purposes. Not long after, on March 21, 1933, the Federal government charged him with income tax evasion. Mitchell had already resigned from the bank because of his revealing testimony and his trial was front-page news. At the trial he was acquitted by the jury, which held that the transactions had been in good faith. This made them legal, and such tax avoidance was not uncommon at that time under the income tax laws then in force.

Wiggin did not get into quite as much trouble as Mitchell but he, too, demonstrated that the laws and ethics of banking were not then what, presumably, they are today. Through personal holding companies which he had set up (two of them named for his daughters) he speculated in the stock of his own bank, financing part of the deal with loans from the bank. He later said it was all right for bank officers to speculate in their own stock because it developed an interest in their institution. At the end of 1932, when his activities had been revealed, Wiggin resigned as chairman of the board.

Another hero whose feet turned out to be made of clay was Richard Whitney, who had once, seemingly almost by himself, stemmed disaster on the stock market. In 1930 he had become president of the New York Stock Exchange. Whitney's own business ventures turned out badly, however; he had to borrow more and more money. Eventually he took to posting securities that were in his custody but belonged to other people, as collateral for his loans. As usual, such actions eventually came to light and in March, 1938, he was arrested on a charge of grand larceny. He went to jail.

The mistakes and misdeeds of two other heroes of the 1920's did not catch up with them until 1932. One of these men was Ivar Kreuger, known as the Swedish Match King. The other was Samuel Insull, the greatest utility-holding-company promoter of them all. Both were featured on the cover of *Time* magazine as financial geniuses. As early as 1913 Kreuger began to build up an international concern to control the match industry. He also used its resources for his own fraudulent purposes, deceiving not only individual investors but also leading investment firms. In March, 1932, when he could no longer juggle his collapsing affairs, he committed suicide. American investors, unprotected by any laws that required the managers of an enterprise to give an honest accounting to their stockholders, had been taken to the extent of a quarter of a billion dollars. Even Harvard University had believed in the Match King.

Insull began his business career as a secretary to the inventor Thomas A. Edison. Moving on to Chicago, he was soon the most powerful man in the Midwest in urban transportation and electric utilities. By organizing mergers and by forming one holding company after another, Insull, at the peak of his and the country's boom, controlled a utilities empire worth more than $3,000,000,000. He became a patron of the arts and gave Chicago a gorgeous opera house. But his empire was built on speculation and when the boom collapsed, so did Insull's over-extended enterprises. He fled to Greece in April, 1932, to escape irate investors who had lost $700,000,000 by believing in him. He was brought back to the United States, tried on charges of embezzlement and of using the mails to defraud—and acquitted.

The stock market crash and its aftermath revealed some sad truths about the nation's economy as well as about the ethics and practices of some of its business leaders. It was a while, though, before the picture became clear. For one thing, the state of the science of collecting and analyzing statistics on a nationwide basis was lamentable compared with the almost overwhelming volume of figures that today come out of government and private sources. There were, for example, almost as many estimates of the increase in unemployment after the stock market collapsed as there were persons or organizations doing the estimating. At first the average person was inclined to see the stock market as the cause of the depression, whereas it was both a symptom and a result of deeper weaknesses. In a sense, the crash caused the depression only to the extent that it destroyed confidence in business and, especially, in the infallibility of the businessman as high priest of a new era.

When available data are examined, they show that economic distress signals appeared months before the stock market caved in. It was in June, 1929, that the Federal Reserve Board index of industrial production reached its peak at 126. Thereafter, it declined month by month and was down to 118 by October. The amount of money put into residential construction declined from $5,000,000,000 to $3,000,000,000 in 1929, and construction is always one of the bulwarks of the economy. The auto industry, in spite of its growth, was no longer growing as fast as it once had. This affected such key industries as steel, glass, and rubber. The government's tax, farm, and tariff policies were all designed—although, of course, those in power did not believe this—to damage the economy by supporting the unsound distribution of the national income and by throwing all possible obstacles in the way of larger and more profitable foreign trade. The banking system was weak and uncoordinated, unsuited to a modern, technological economy that spread over a continent. Almost 7,000 banks failed during the 1920's. The average person began to spend less for consumer goods, although for a while this fact was hidden by an increase in buying on the installment plan. When hard times came, this merely aggravated the situation since families could not find the money to pay the installment collector. Looking back, it seems as though the economists and government employees interpreted statistics and advised business and government to take exactly those steps best calculated to make things worse.

One estimate placed the number of unemployed in October, 1929, at about 1,500,000 people. By early 1930 more than 4,000,000 men and women were out of work, and this was out of a total civilian work force of only about two-thirds as many persons as there are today. Even so, as 1929 came to a close, most economists, government officials, and business leaders refused to believe that any serious economic crisis was upon the nation. Many reassuring statements were issued and solemnly printed by the newspapers. There were those, including Secretary of the Treasury Mellon, who believed that a depression, like an illness, had to run its course and that the only thing to do was to suffer with a stiff upper lip until the economic fever had passed. This was easier for a millionaire like Mr. Mellon than for the factory worker who had already lost his job.

President Hoover was not quite as optimistic; nor did he agree with his Secretary of the Treasury that economic nature should be allowed to take its course no matter how many suffered. On the other hand, he believed that while the Federal government should advise and encourage voluntary efforts to stem the decline, it should not step in directly by, for example, spending Federal money for the relief of individuals. He first resorted to one of his favorite devices, a series of conferences of business, labor, and community leaders. He persuaded a number of the top managers of large industries to promise not to cut wages. He announced an income tax reduction, which was a step in the right direction. However, since rates were unbelievably low compared with what they are today, the result was more psychological than financial. A man with an income of $4,000 a year had his tax cut from $5.63 to $1.88.

As the 1920's came to an end and the 1930's began, there were many expressions of optimism from what were, supposedly, the best business and financial brains of the country. Somewhat more cautiously, the White House reported that the President considered "business could look forward to the coming year with greater assurance." From the White House down, the men in power had not long to wait to discover just how completely wrong they were.

3 *From Bad to Worse*

As 1930 OPENED scarcely anyone believed the nation had already entered a long depression. Business leaders were as ignorant about the future as the man in the street. Charles M. Schwab, a leading steel manufacturer who had been the first president of U.S. Steel, said that "all present indications are that 1930, in broad perspective, will prove to be a year of normal business progress." Even if the stock market collapse heralded a depression, surely, most people thought, it could not last long. Was not the United States a rich nation? We could produce all the food, clothing, shelter, and, as well, all the autos, movies, and radios the nation needed or wanted. As the depression deepened this became the great paradox: food rotting while people starved; farmers losing their farms because they produced too much food; modern textile factories shut down while people needed clothing to keep warm. In earlier eras hard times had meant an actual shortage of goods, even of food. In the new-style depression one could starve in the midst of plenty.

In January, 1930, a poll by the National Economic League showed that those queried thought the three most important problems facing the nation were the administration of justice, prohibition, and lawlessness. Unemployment ranked only eighteenth. Two years later, when conditions were much worse, a similar poll put economy and efficiency in government at the top of the list while unemployment still ranked no more than tenth. Later in 1930 anyone who watched the various economic statistics and indices should have begun to worry. With the 1935–39 average as 100, the Federal Reserve Board's index of industrial production stood at 91 in 1930 and slumped to 75 the next year. While about 5,500,000 autos and trucks had been manufactured in 1929, the figure declined by about 2,100,000 in 1930. Factories began to reduce their production and then to close. Between 1923 and 1931 the depressed textile industry shut down 30 per cent of the spindles in its factories in the South.

Perhaps most ominous of all was the increase in bank failures. In 1929, 659 American banks had failed; in 1930 the number rose to 1,352 and in 1931 to 2,294. Just before Christmas, 1930, the Bank of the United States in New York City collapsed. It had 400,000 depositors, many of them recent immigrants, and its failure, the worst in the country's history, affected a third of all the people of the city. A bank panic in the Middle South closed 129 banks. As usual, people began to withdraw their money and it is estimated that by 1931 they had taken $1,000,000,000 from the care of the bankers and had hidden it away in everything from safe deposit boxes to old mattresses. And just at the time when the people were losing jobs and money, states and other governmental units imposed new taxes to make up for declining revenues from other sources. Thus the depression was chiefly responsible for the introduction of the sales tax, Kentucky being the first state to have one, in 1930. Other states and cities followed suit.

Somewhat deceptively, wages did not decline much for about a year after the crash. President Hoover's attempt to keep wages up by voluntary effort worked for a while. Then smaller firms in competitive industries began to cut wage rates. As consumer demand slowed down, fewer hours of work were needed to produce the goods that could be sold, so that even if the hourly rate was not cut, a week's wages totaled fewer dollars. For a while, real wages—take-home money judged in terms of what it would buy—were partly sustained because the cost of living was also going down.

The dam broke in September, 1931, when U.S. Steel announced it would reduce wage rates by 10 per cent on October 1. General Motors, U. S. Rubber, and others followed and the self-appointed champion of high wages, Henry Ford, cut the pay of his men by more than 10 per cent. Civil service workers in many government units had their salaries reduced. The railroad unions agreed with management on a 10 per cent cut, although it was not to take effect until February 1, 1932.

As early as the fall of 1930, when wages began to go down and unemployment continued to go up, President Hoover appointed a committee to head off disaster by voluntary cooperation. Colonel Arthur Woods, businessman and former New York City police commissioner, was named to head the President's Emergency Committee for Employment (PECE). The PECE had no power, almost no money, and was to rely on persuasion and optimism. It urged Hoover to support a larger Federal construction program, including $600,000,000 for highways. The President did not think this would be financially prudent. The PECE urged employers to give work to more men by having each man work fewer hours. It urged cities and nongovernmental organizations to provide relief for the unemployed, but the job was rapidly getting to be more than private charity could cope with.

The farm situation was becoming worse as wholesale prices for food products went downhill rapidly. To add to their other woes, farmers were afflicted by drought conditions in 1930, especially in the Mississippi and Ohio valleys and in the whole Southwest. The prices the farmer received went downhill so rapidly that between 1929 and 1932 net farm income dropped to less than a third of what it had been. But the farmer's taxes and debts, especially the mortgage on his farm, remained at the high level of the 1920's.

Congress, meanwhile, was working on a new tariff bill which became law in June, 1930, as the Hawley-Smoot Tariff, and did its part to aggravate the depression. It once again raised duties on imports of both agricultural and industrial products. It thus increased prices for American consumers, reduced foreign trade in general, and made it more difficult for farmers and manufacturers to sell their products abroad because other nations retaliated. Within two years twenty-five other countries raised their rates against American imports. More than 1,000 members of the American Economic Association petitioned President Hoover to veto the bill, but he signed it into law.

The United States was hit earlier and harder by depression than the rest of the world, but it was not alone in its suffering. The effects of World War I were still being felt, and the burden of the huge reparations which Germany was ordered to pay by the Peace Conference of 1919 was a threat to economic prosperity, no matter how justifiable it seemed to those who had suffered from German aggression. At first President Hoover felt we had only ourselves to blame for what had happened to America. As time went on, though, he began to place more and more of the blame on foreign countries, saying in June, 1931, that "a large part of the forces which have swept our shores from abroad are the malign inheritances in Europe of the Great War. . . ."

Disaster struck in Europe in the spring of 1931 and it had its repercussions in the United States. In May the Kreditanstalt, Austria's largest bank, failed and Austria went off the gold standard. Financial trouble spread to Germany, Rumania, and Hungary. Business conditions were already bad in Germany and political discontent, fanned by the Nazis, was on the rise. In June a positive step, involving war debts and reparations, was taken under President

Hoover's leadership. After World War I, when the final accounting was in, the allies of the United States owed us nearly $10,500,000,000. In turn, Germany owed the allies (excluding the United States, which did not participate in these reparations payments) $33,000,000,000. It soon became apparent that the only way Germany could pay this enormous sum was to borrow from American bankers. And only if Germany paid the allies could England, France, Italy, and Belgium pay their war debts to the United States. Twice already, in 1925 under the Dawes Plan and in 1929 under the Young Plan, the reparations sum had been cut to meet reality. Now Hoover proposed a moratorium for one year, during which time Germany would not be expected to pay the allies and they would not be expected to pay us. Some of the effect of the moratorium was spoiled by France's reluctant agreement to go along. As it turned out, this moratorium for practical purposes was the end of the payments for good.

England had weathered the onset of the depression fairly well except for a sharp drop in exports. To some extent, though, appearances were deceiving because England had had continued economic troubles since the end of the war, especially in coal mining and cotton manufacturing where facilities were obsolete. However, the trouble in central Europe hit England hard because of her financial involvements. In August, 1931, the three major political parties formed a national government as business and financial difficulties increased. On September 21 England was forced to go off the gold standard. This meant that the value of the pound, which had been the world standard among currencies for about a century, dropped considerably. To some extent this aided Britain by lowering the cost of her exports to those who wished to buy them. Unemployment had reached 2,000,000 by mid-1930 and was up another half-million at the start of 1931. There was much more unemployment in Germany, while France was relatively the best off of these three major nations.

In 1931, too, both the British Empire and the doctrine of free trade came officially to an end. By the Statute of Westminster, an act of Parliament, the leading dependencies were recognized as independent and equal dominions, joined to the United Kingdom only by common allegiance to the crown. On the business side, one step to fight the depression was to impose for the first time in nearly a century tariffs on imports into the United Kingdom, but the dominions and the colonies of the Commonwealth got preferential treatment. Canada felt the depression along with the Commonwealth and the United States. Her trade with the latter suffered, of course, while as an exporter of raw materials she found the prices of such things dropped faster and farther than almost anything else.

At home the American people were more concerned in 1930 and 1931 with their private economic troubles than with those of Europe and other parts of the world. The number of people moving to the city from the farm began to decline. There were no jobs in the cities but perhaps on the land one could grow enough to eat. There was even a sizable increase, for a while, of people moving back to the farm from the city, but many missed the glamour of the city and found it wasn't as easy to grow one's own food as it seemed. A new group of wandering transients came into being, people, including many youths, who traveled aimlessly from one state to another by hitching rides or hopping freight trains. By 1933 there may have been as many as a million of them. Marriage rates and birth rates dropped rapidly. The result was noticeable later, in the 1950's, when the number of young men and women reaching the first-job age was unusually small. Immigration from other countries almost ceased and in 1931, for the first time in the history of the country, more people left it than came in.

The bankers and the speculators all over the world may have lost their millions, but ordinary people were losing something much more vital—their jobs. While unemployment in the United States had reached 4,000,000 as early as the start of 1930, it doubled in the course of the year; and by the end of 1931 more than 9,000,000 Americans, most of them dependent on week-to-week wages and salaries, were without any income of that kind. About one of every six persons who wanted to work was already unable to find a job.

What did these people do? Some of them kept trudging from factory to factory and employment office to employment office, often on shoes whose soles were worn through, hoping that some day there would again be a job for them. Some gradually sank into apathy, defeated by the world and ashamed of their condition, for there lingered the old saying, used mostly by those who didn't need a job, that "anyone who really wants a job can always find one." There are even stories of men who left their homes as usual each morning and returned each evening, traveling as they previously had, even though they no longer had an office to go to. When Soviet Russia announced there were available in that country jobs for 6,000 skilled workers, over 100,000 Americans applied. Actually, economic conditions in the only Communist nation were not as rosy as this offer implied. Men begged to serve on juries instead of trying to avoid their civic duty as they had once done—because it paid comparatively well. Hundreds of males of all ages, from boys to old men, in large cities took up shoe shining—at a time when fewer people could afford shoeshines even at the cut price of five cents.

Best remembered from depression days are the apple sellers who in the fall of 1930 turned up at street corners everywhere. The International Apple Shippers' Association, faced with a surplus, offered to let unemployed men have apples on credit at wholesale prices. The apple sellers, who shivered through the 1930–31 winter and who are supposed to have included ruined bankers and brokers, asked only a nickel for apples that today sell for about three times that amount. As recently as March, 1966, a cartoon in a New York newspaper, showing several elderly gentlemen talking in front of a fruit stand with apples prominently displayed, had one of them saying: "Let's discuss the roaring bull market somewhere else."

America had a long tradition of neighborliness and of charity and philanthropy. Unfortunately, there was also a belief that aid to the poor encouraged laziness and destroyed morale. At the most, if private charity was not sufficient, it was up to each municipality to care for its own. As the depression worsened in 1930, the towns and cities were less able than ever to care for their needy; nor were people on the whole as able as before to give to private charity. Still, President Hoover insisted that the Federal government should not spend money for the relief of individual citizens. When the 1930 drought brought disaster to farmers, Hoover urged Congress to appropriate money to be loaned to the farmers to buy such things as seed and cattle feed. His opponents taunted him that he was willing to feed cattle but not people.

Meanwhile more and more people were without funds and, so, without food, except for charity, begging, and picking over the refuse of restaurants and city dumps. Newspaper reporters, social workers, and authors such as Thomas Wolfe and Edmund Wilson have all left harrowing, and often bitter, accounts of human scavengers. Lillian Wald of the Henry Street Settlement in New York asked: "Have you ever heard a hungry child cry? Have you seen the uncontrollable trembling of parents who have gone half starved for weeks so that the children may have food?" Investigating conditions in Chicago, Wilson wrote: "There is not a garbage-dump in Chicago which is not diligently haunted by the hungry." The young novelist Thomas Wolfe, coming north, was appalled: ". . . the unending repercussions of these scenes of suffering, violence, oppression, hunger, cold, and the filth and poverty going on unheeded in a world in which the rich were still rotten with their wealth, left a scar upon my life." That such writings were not merely the exaggerations of the literary world is shown, perhaps, by one statistic such as this: in 1931 four New York City hospitals reported ninety-five cases of starvation.

In August, 1931, President Hoover appointed another committee. This one was known as the President's Organization on Unemployment Relief (POUR), or the Gifford Committee, for its chairman, Walter S. Gifford, president of the American Telephone and Telegraph Company. Its main effort was to support, by modern advertising techniques, the efforts of local charitable agencies to raise money. It was of little help and, as its chairman later admitted at a Senate hearing, it did not even collect any figures on what was needed or what was available for relief.

At first the states and the cities did not do much either. New York City, with an inept and corrupt government, tried to get along until early 1931 on private charity but by then the city had to be forced into a special appropriation for relief work. Soup kitchens and breadlines sprang up all over the city, feeding many but also exposing them to the humiliation of standing in long lines for a handout. By January, 1931, there were 82 breadlines serving 85,000 meals a day. In the Times Square area there were breadlines and theater ticket lines at the same time.

By the summer of 1931 the states had to step in, led by New York. Here, under Governor Roosevelt's leadership, a Temporary Emergency Relief Administration was set up with $20,000,000 to be distributed through the counties and cities. Its first executive director was Harry L. Hopkins, who began an association with Franklin Roosevelt that was to become closer and closer and was to end only with Roosevelt's death. New Jersey, Rhode Island, and other states gradually made similar appropriations. It was none too soon. By the fall of 1931 Chicago had 624,000 unemployed and an incompetent and bankrupt government. The situation in Detroit was perhaps worst of all. There was tremendous unemployment because the auto industry was so hard hit, while no group showed less civic responsibility than the great motor magnates who had discharged thousands of men. At this period relief payments to a whole family in New York City were only $2.39 a week, and it was less almost everywhere else.

There was one small bright spot in the situation which would benefit the nation in later years. The depression gave impetus to social work as a profession. In 1930 there were 40,000 social workers but by 1940 this number was about doubled.

Unemployment and the distress resulting from it were bound to lead to unrest. The wonder of it now, looking back, is that there was so little of it and that most of it was mild. In Oklahoma City in January, 1931, a crowd of men and women, out of work and hungry, raided a grocery store near city hall. About a month later several hundred people in Minneapolis attacked a grocery and meat market, helping themselves to food. But these and others were exceptional incidents. The deteriorating economic situation did, however, give the Communists, directed from Moscow, a chance to try to take advantage of the situation.

First organized in 1919 as a result of the Communist take-over in Russia but divided most of the time by endless hair-splitting disputes over Marxist doctrine, the Communist party in the United States had about 6,000 members in 1930. Two years later, in spite of assistance from the economic storm, the number had no more than doubled. The chief Communist leaders for a number of years—although at times each was out of favor with the men in Moscow who really ran the party—were Earl Browder and William Z. Foster. The former was a quiet, soft-spoken Kansan who was the Communist candidate for the presidency in 1936 and 1940 and who acted not at all like the bearded bomb-throwing Bolsheviks of the newspaper cartoons. Foster, also native born, was an older radical labor leader, best known for his leadership of the steel strike of 1919.

Although they were few in number, the Communists were well trained and fanatically dedicated and energetic. They spent a great deal of their time leading non-Communists in demonstrations and strikes. They joined labor unions and other organizations and by sheer tenacity often carried far more weight than their numbers deserved. The depression was a godsend to them. Their most dramatic effort in the early depression years was a National Hunger March on Washington, which they stage-managed in December, 1931. The plan called for nearly 1,200 truckloads of demonstrators to converge on the capital, but only 71 trucks were needed. The marchers were met by a force of police that must have outnumbered them, and after a march on Capitol Hill they left the city, much to the relief of some public officials who seem to have been more nervous than they needed to be.

In Cleveland in February, 1930, Communist leaders incited about 3,000 unemployed persons to march on city hall. Next month they proclaimed March 6 International Unemployment Day with demonstrations in most of the large cities. Some of these were broken up by the police with considerable violence. Edmund Wilson's description of a Communist-led "hunger march" on New York's city hall could apply to most such events. There were the demonstrators: "mostly small scrubby zealous people wearing red neckties, red hats or red dresses. A good many of the women have glasses." They carried banners and placards, they listened to speaker after speaker until the police charged in, broke up the meeting, and cracked a few heads as well. The Communist organizers would have been unhappy if the police ("Cossacks") had not done so.

The Communists also stepped into court trials where, quite apart from the question of seeing justice done, they thought they could propagandize for their movement. The most famous case in the 1930's was the Scottsboro trial, which began in March, 1931, when nine (one was soon released because of his age) Negro youths were arrested on charges of having raped two white girls. They, together with others—whites and Negroes of both sexes—had been riding a freight train in the South. Within less than two weeks, in Scottsboro, Alabama, the eight were tried and sentenced to death. The agitation of the Communists, as well as the efforts of many others who believed justice had been miscarried, made the case internationally known. Trials and retrials and hearings and appeals up to the United States Supreme Court went on for many years. None of the accused was executed and in 1948 the last of the eight still in jail escaped.

Contrary to Marxist theory, communism in the United States during the depression had less appeal to the jobless, hungry workers than it did to writers and other intellectuals. In part this may have been the result of feelings of guilt. In any event, while not very many of them joined the party, a good many aided it in one way or another. For many whose faith in democracy and capitalism had been shaken, communism offered a new hope. They were strongly influenced by the *Autobiography* (1931) of Lincoln Steffens, the much respected author and reformer who had visited Soviet Russia and who thought he saw the future shape of the world there. Two years later John Strachey's *The Coming Struggle for Power* convinced many that communism would succeed where capitalism appeared to have failed. Others were influenced by their own observations, such as novelist Theodore Dreiser's investigation of conditions in Harlan County, Kentucky, where miners and mine owners were waging almost open warfare.

Many who had been liberal or mildly Socialist were drawn to communism as the depression worsened. Such a man was Granville Hicks, a Harvard graduate with a middle-class background. He became a leading literary critic and editor of the radical magazine *The New Masses*. He grew disillusioned with communism and resigned from the party in 1939. Michael Gold (born Irving Granich on New York's Lower East Side) was more directly the proletarian intellectual. He too became an editor of *The New Masses.* In the terminology of the times, men such as these wrote proletarian literature, which was based on the Marxist theory that everything is conditioned by social and economic factors and that an author can understand his environment only by applying Marxist principles. In practice this meant that in the 1930's there were a good many novels with working-class settings and characters, including Gold's *Jews Without Money* (1930), Albert Halper's *The Foundry* (1934), and Grace Lumpkin's *To Make My Bread* (1932).

The Communist movement continued to grow during the 1930's, but after the New Deal came into power in 1933, there was again a channel through which many who wanted to improve and reform the social and economic system could do so within the traditional American framework, access to which had been denied them by a dozen years of Republicanism in power.

As time went on, many who in the early thirties had worked with the Communists withdrew their support. Some of the younger ones simply grew older and changed their views, as happens with every generation. Some of the older ones became disillusioned with the party's doctrinaire attitude and rigid discipline that stifled independent thinking. Most of those who became sympathetic to communism at this time had done so, not because they had suddenly come to believe in and love Marxism, but simply because the times were so discouraging and the old ways seemed so useless.

Politics did not take a vacation because of the depression. As a matter of fact, political activity and partisanship were stimulated. Nor did the world as a whole remain quiet while economic distress ran its course; rather, there were indications of trouble abroad, along with attempts to make permanent the hard-won peace.

The voters' first chance to assess President Hoover's handling of the depression came in the fall of 1930 when one-third of the Senate and all of the House of Representatives were chosen. As a result of the 1928 election the Republicans had been firmly in power with a majority of about 100 in the House and with 56 of the 96 senators. In 1930 the voters expressed their displeasure with the state of the Union by giving the Democrats control of the House by a small margin and leaving the Republicans with exactly half of the Senate. In practice, several progressive Republican senators were as anti-Hoover as any of the Democrats. Dissatisfaction with the administration in Washington was also shown in a number of states where Democrats took over the governors' chairs. Most significantly, Franklin D. Roosevelt, who had been elected governor of New York in 1928 by only 25,000 votes, won re-election in a smashing landslide that gave him a 700,000-vote majority.

By the 1930's Americans had become cynical about World War I, keeping up the tradition that we were innocent and had to beware of the Old World's wickedness. Isolationism was growing. Even so, the United States was participating in international conferences and treaties more than it ever had before, especially in those which, it was believed, would make another war impossible. The country had taken the lead in starting a series of meetings intended to limit naval armaments. The first had been held in 1921–22 in Washington, and now in 1930 a second was held in London. In both conferences the three major naval powers—Great Britain, Japan, and the United States—had agreed to ratios among them; for example, Japan agreed to build no more than three capital ships to each five for England and America. The situation looked bright in 1930 but in 1934 Japan announced it would withdraw from the pacts. A conference the next year to try to win Japan back to armament control ended when the Japanese withdrew from the meeting. Naval disarmament was dead. One sidelight of the 1930 conference was not much noted: for the first time radio newsmen as well as newspapermen accompanied the United States delegation.

It was the Japanese, also, who took the first warlike action of the decade. In September, 1931, their troops invaded, and soon controlled, Manchuria. From the American point of view this was a violation of the League of Nations Covenant, the Nine-Power Treaty, and the Kellogg-Briand Pact. Secretary of State Henry L. Stimson would have liked to take action, such as economic sanctions, against Japan. The rest of the world showed little interest and the American people were in no mood to fight over Manchuria. In January, 1932, Stimson, in a well-meaning but futile gesture, announced that the United States would not recognize the legality of such actions. In Germany Adolf Hitler, not yet in power, probably took note.

At home, Americans, to the extent their pocketbooks and their worries about hard times permitted, were carrying on much as before the stock market crash. Prohibition and crime, closely linked, figured prominently in the news. In January, 1931, the Wickersham Commission which Hoover had appointed in 1929 made its report to the nation. It found that criminal law was being inadequately enforced. As to prohibition, the Commission seemed to say that it was unenforceable but that it should be enforced. There was one big triumph for justice that year. Al Capone, who in a decade of lawlessness and brutality in Chicago had become the epitome of the rich and powerful American gangster, went to jail. However, he did not go for murder, bootlegging, labor union racketeering, vice, or any other crime one thought of when his name was mentioned. He was sentenced to eleven years in jail for evading his Federal income tax. By the time he emerged in 1939 he was broken in health and through as a criminal power.

In the transportation field, the railroads suffered not only from the depression but also from the competition of the automobile and the airplane. Although, in the course of the period, the rail lines cut their passenger fares, gradually introduced air-conditioned cars, and began to retire the steam locomotive in favor of the diesel engine, they nevertheless lost ground. Hard times slowed the pace of the auto industry, but passenger cars and buses took passengers away from the rails, while trucks began to haul an impressive share of the nation's freight. In 1930 the railroads carried 708,000,000 passengers; in a quarter of a century the number dropped by nearly 300,000,000.

At the start of the decade most flying was still for the fun of it, but commercial air transport was beginning. In 1930 Charles A. Lindbergh, who had thrilled the world with his solo flight from New York to Paris in 1927, with his wife set a transcontinental record of fourteen and three-quarters hours. The next year Wiley Post and Harold Gatty flew around the world in eight days and fifteen hours to establish a new record. And in 1930 the first airline stewardess, a girl named Ellen Church, went to work.

Some of the largest and noblest construction projects the country has ever seen were finished after the depression set in. An outstanding example was the Empire State Building, erected on Fifth Avenue in New York City on the site of the old Waldorf-Astoria Hotel, which at this same time built itself a new and grander home fifteen blocks uptown on Park Avenue. Officially opened on May 1, 1931, the Empire State Building was 1,250 feet high, boasted 102 stories, and took the title of world's tallest building away from the still-new Chrysler Building. Al Smith was president of the company that owned the building, but even his name could not fill it with tenants. It was not long before many of the elevators were shut down because whole floors were empty. An even more grandiose office-building project was Rockefeller Center, planned by the Rockefeller family to include radio and the arts. Originally the Metropolitan

Opera was to have a new home in this development, but it turned out to be a full generation before the Met moved anywhere. The National Broadcasting Company became one of the main tenants, and part of the project, including the seventy-story RCA Building, was soon familiarly known as Radio City. Between 1931 and 1939, fourteen buildings were erected, including the one housing the Radio City Music Hall. The original intention was to present in it live shows only, but the depression soon put an end to that and the Music Hall had to content itself with being the biggest movie theater of all. Still farther uptown, and also built with Rockefeller money, the Riverside Church opened in 1930. It was planned for its pastor, the Reverend Harry Emerson Fosdick. His was the most eloquent pulpit voice of the time and, in keeping with the state of the world, he dealt much more with personal problems than with theology.

The largest bridge of the era, and one of the most beautiful of any era, was opened in October, 1931. This was the George Washington Bridge over the Hudson River between New York and New Jersey. Work had begun in 1927 on the bridge whose main span is 3,500 feet long. Out west on the Colorado River work on the Hoover Dam began in 1931 and was finished in 1936. One of the largest dams ever built, it is 726 feet high, 1,244 feet long; and Lake Mead, which it created, is 115 miles long.

Literature had a better two years in 1930–31 than did business. In 1930 Sinclair Lewis, whose books up to then had satirized the smug Americans of the prosperous twenties, became the first American to win the Nobel Prize for literature. In tune with the changed times was *The 42nd Parallel* by John Dos Passos, the first novel of a trilogy that emphasized the crass commercialism of America in the twentieth century. Dos Passos never joined the Communist party but he was one of the leading "fellow travelers" among important literary figures until he became disenchanted by the Communists' "unintelligent fanaticism," as he put it.

Most Americans read for relaxation and escape during the thirties, although there was a comparatively large market for books dealing with current problems. Detective stories reached the height of their popularity at this time, especially as the "hard-boiled" style came to the fore. Its leading exponent was Dashiell Hammett, whose best-known book, *The Maltese Falcon,* was published in 1930. The first of the very popular Perry Mason stories was published in 1933. For style and traditional upper-class settings, though, the English mystery writers were never topped, especially Agatha Christie and Dorothy Sayers. With more leisure and less money, readers made more use of libraries, both the free public type and the rental libraries operated by bookstores. Through the latter, one could, for a few cents a day, read the latest novel or nonfiction best seller, but in not much more than a decade the paperback book put the lending libraries into a decline. Typical of the beginning of the thirties were such books as *The Good Earth,* by Pearl Buck; *Arundel,* by Kenneth Roberts; and *Shadows on the Rock,* by Willa Cather.

If no great music was being written in America at this time, at least it was now possible for everyone to listen to the best music of the ages. Thanks to radio, the Metropolitan Opera's Saturday afternoon performances could be heard, beginning in 1931, while the New York Philharmonic Orchestra's Sunday afternoon concerts were first broadcast in 1930. The "Ford Sunday Evening Hour" of music was one of the most popular programs on the air. It was a wonderful time for popular music and for dancing to the slow, sweet music of the "big bands," such as those of Guy Lombardo, Wayne King, Eddy Duchin, Vincent Lopez, Fred Waring, and Rudy Vallee, with his theme song "The Maine Stein Song." Two other theme songs made their debuts in 1931—Kate Smith's "When the Moon Comes Over the Mountain" and Bing Crosby's "When the Blue of the Night Meets the Gold of the Day." Other hits of 1930–31 that are still heard today include "Dancing in the Dark," "Goodnight Sweetheart," "Body and Soul," "Beyond the Blue Horizon," and "I Got Rhythm."

In 1931 the most popular show on Broadway was *Of Thee I Sing,* with music by George Gershwin, lyrics by his brother Ira, and book by George S. Kaufman and Morrie Ryskind. Even though it was a satire of American politics at a time of crisis in the nation's history, the staid Pulitzer Prize judges the next year gave it their drama award. On the whole the Broadway theater was not faring well. By 1931 two-thirds of the theaters were shut down. As usual, a few hits were extremely popular, such as *Green Pastures* in 1930 and *The Barretts of Wimpole Street,* with Katharine Cornell, in 1931. That year the most talked-about play was Eugene O'Neill's *Mourning Becomes Electra,* long enough for three ordinary plays.

Radio-listening became more popular than ever. If one had a set, staying home and listening was the cheapest form of entertainment available. And the business and entertainment worlds were combining to bring more information and amusement to the home than ever. Two out of every five homes had a radio and the first attempts to find out who in those homes was listening to which programs began with the Crossley ratings, which made use of phone calls to survey the radio audience. In 1930–31 there was something for everyone: a cat-and-dog fight was heard; Gene Autry aired his first program, for which he got $50 a week; commentator H. V. Kaltenborn joined CBS; the "Damrosch Music Appreciation Hour" on NBC was heard in thousands of schools; short-wave broadcasting brought to the United States the voices of the playwright George Bernard Shaw, the Italian dictator Benito Mussolini, and the Indian independence leader Mahatma Gandhi.

In the field of mass entertainment, only the movies could compete with radio. In 1930 more than 100,000,000 tickets a week were purchased at movie box offices at a time when the total population was about 123,000,000. In those days one could get into almost any movie at almost any time of the day for less than a dollar. To attract more customers in bad times, the movies introduced double features in 1931. There were many good movies to see: *All Quiet on the Western Front,* perhaps the best war movie ever made; *Little Caesar,* the first gangster film and the first step in Edward G. Robinson's career; *The Dawn Patrol,* in which Douglas Fairbanks, Jr., was very brave; *Hell's Angels,* which made a star overnight of Jean Harlow; *Frankenstein,* which made a successful monster out of Boris Karloff; *The Front Page,* Pat O'Brien's first picture; *Public Enemy,* in which James Cagney demonstrated it was all right to be tough with ladies; and *Monkey Business,* one of the Marx Brothers' comedies that helped make the depression bearable.

Americans did not lose their interest in sports during the depression, although a million or more had to give up membership in golf clubs, while sales of sporting goods dropped by half. The athletic hero of 1930 was an amateur golfer, Bobby Jones, who achieved the grand slam of the game. He won the U.S. Open and Amateur championships and the British Open and Amateur, a feat never yet repeated. By this time Jones had won thirteen major titles. For most people, the nearest they came to matching Jones's efforts was to play miniature golf, a fad that swept the country in 1930. By September there were 30,000 miniature golf courses in operation and their owners had invested $125,000,000 in them. For a dime or so, one could play a round of golf with a putter over a small course of artificial grass, tin pipes, and other obstacles. Millions of people flocked to college football stadiums on Saturdays but the excitement wasn't quite as frantic as it had been in the Jazz Age. The best-known coach, Knute Rockne, of the best-known team, the University of Notre Dame, was killed at the age of forty-three in an airplane crash in March, 1931. A portent of different times to come was the first snow train, run by a New England railroad in 1930.

Among indoor sports, contract bridge was popular enough to

amount to a craze. The sale of playing cards was one thing that did not go down during the depression, and Ely Culbertson, the most heeded authority on bridge, estimated that in 1931 Americans paid out $10,000,000 for bridge lessons. In late 1931 Culbertson and his wife played two other experts, Sidney Lenz and Oswald Jacoby, in a match that received front-page coverage from the newspapers.

There were millions of other things going on in the United States in which the people participated or took an interest. They already had 20,200,000 telephones (today there are nearly five times as many). Over them Americans could talk about the Irish Sweepstakes, which began in 1930, or "Monopoly," a game which had just become popular and has remained so ever since. American women bought 300,000,000 pairs of silk stockings (there was no such thing as nylon yet) compared with 12,000 pairs in 1900. On August 6 a New York judge named Crater disappeared and his whereabouts have never been discovered. In 1931 Winston Churchill was hit by an automobile on Fifth Avenue. The silly season craze that year was tree-sitting, with contestants trying to see who could stay up among the leaves and branches the longest. New York City subway and bus fares were only a nickel, except for the Fifth Avenue buses which cost a dime. But these buses had a conductor who came around to collect the fare, as well as a driver, and they were double-deckers. In the summer the top decks were open-air, and one could ride all the way from Washington Square to upper Manhattan for ten cents, breezes included. It was at this time in the nation's history, too, that the sales of glass jars for home canning of fruits and vegetables were the highest in a decade.

This was America at the end of 1931, foundering ever deeper in depression, doing little about it, and still trying to carry on as normally as possible.

4 *The Coming of FDR*

THE YEAR 1932 WAS THE DARKEST, dreariest, most disastrous year of the Great Depression. Unemployment went up another 3,000,000 or 4,000,000—no one was quite sure—to around 13,000,000. In New York City 1,000,000 people were out of jobs. In some cities 80 per cent of the workers were unemployed. The giant steel plants of the country were operating at only about an eighth of their full capacity. The Gross National Product (the sum of all the goods and services produced in the country) had been $104,000,000,000 in 1929 but it fell by almost half in 1932 to only $58,500,000,000. It was understandable that many people were rather annoyed when it was revealed that by legal ingenuity J. P. Morgan, the financier's financier, had not paid a cent of Federal income tax for three years.

One phenomenon of the time was the establishment of "Hoovervilles" on empty lots and around the outskirts of cities. These ramshackle communities of hastily-thrown-together shacks housed thousands of homeless, jobless, moneyless men. St. Louis had a very large one, but the Hooverville with the best location was the one established in Central Park in New York City. It was familiarly known as Hoover Valley and the shanties were built in the bed of an old reservoir. In September, 1932, the police somewhat apologetically raided Hoover Valley and arrested twenty-five men on charges of vagrancy.

The number of men, women, and children dependent on charity or public relief funds increased alarmingly and the cities were less able than ever to carry the load. The Lynds tell in *Middletown* how its township costs for relief rose from $21,000 in 1928 to nearly $300,000 in 1932; the number of families on relief rose from 613 to 3,036—every fourth family. Chicago not only had no relief money, it was unable to pay its own employees for long periods. Hospitals in New York reported an increase in rickets among children because of undernourishment. When the city of Birmingham advertised temporary jobs for 750 men, 12,000 applied. Finally, President Hoover realized that only the Federal government could avert further disaster. In July the Emergency Relief Act became law, authorizing the national government to lend up to $300,000,000 to the states for relief purposes. The magnitude of the problem was at last being recognized.

Those on the farms were faring no better. Farm prices fell and fell still more. Wheat that sold for $1.05 a bushel in 1929 brought the farmer only 39 cents by 1932; corn was down from 81 cents to 33 cents a bushel; cotton from 17 cents to 6 cents a pound. By the summer of 1932 some farmers were ready for direct action. In Iowa a Farm Holiday Association, led by Milo Reno, blocked the highways to Sioux City, trying to persuade other farmers not to take their produce to market. Similar action took place elsewhere and in several localities the milk of farmers who refused to join the movement was dumped in the road. Judges who were supposed to auction off farms for the failure of their owners to pay taxes or mortgages were threatened with violence. While all this relieved the farmers' feelings and called attention to their plight, it brought few immediate benefits.

Violence also broke out on the industrial front. On March 7 a crowd of about 3,000 people took part in a Communist-organized "hunger march" against the main Ford auto plant. Starting in

Detroit, they marched toward Dearborn where the plant was located. The Dearborn police ordered them to turn back. The marchers pressed on; the police used tear gas; the demonstrators threw rocks and frozen dirt (the temperature was around zero that day). Eventually the police fired their guns, killing four persons and wounding about fifty. The demonstration was over but the Communists capitalized on it by staging an elaborate funeral for the victims.

Even more ominous was the Bonus Army of 1932 and its "invasion" of Washington, D.C. The origin of this unusual event can be traced to 1924, when Congress passed an Adjusted Compensation Act that gave about 3,500,000 veterans of World War I insurance policies whose value was based on the number of days a man had served in the armed forces. The law provided that payment would be made in 1945, but by 1932 there was a strong demand from the veterans that the face value of the policies be paid in cash right then. In the spring a group of veterans in far-off Oregon, under the leadership of Walter Waters, an unemployed cannery superintendent, decided to travel to the capital to press Congress for payment of the "bonus." The idea caught hold and soon men from all parts of the country, some of them with wives and children, were heading for Washington by car, or on foot, or by hopping onto railroad freight cars. Eventually there were about 20,000 people camped on the mud flats of the Potomac River and using some condemned government buildings on Pennsylvania Avenue.

The superintendent of police, General Pelham D. Glassford, used tact and common sense to keep the restless men from causing trouble. He helped them with food and sanitation problems. Even when the Senate defeated a bill to pay the bonus, the BEF (for Bonus Expeditionary Force) quietly left the area of the Capitol building. Many began to go home but several thousand remained. Hoover continued to refuse to meet with the leaders but he did sponsor a bill to lend the veterans money for transportation. Finally, on July 28, the District of Columbia government ordered Glassford to evict the veterans from the government buildings. At this point a few Communists, who had tried unsuccessfully to get into the leadership of the BEF, attempted to start a riot. They didn't succeed, but a little later a policeman or two became rattled and began firing their pistols, killing two veterans. At this point Hoover, with the advice of other high officials, ordered the U.S. Army to drive out the veterans. Soon infantry, cavalry, tanks, and machine guns were on the way, led by the Chief of Staff himself, faultlessly uniformed General Douglas MacArthur. He was assisted by two officers who were later to fight bigger battles—Dwight D. Eisenhower and George S. Patton, Jr. The soldiers, with bayonets and tear gas, routed the unarmed men, women, and children, and set fire to their miserable shacks. The battle was over and the bonus army scattered. The bonus was finally paid in June, 1936.

The most positive action Hoover took to try to stem the tide of the depression was to suggest the establishment of the Reconstruction Finance Corporation. He proposed it at the end of 1931 and Congress passed the necessary legislation before the end of January, 1932. The RFC was empowered to lend up to $2,000,000,000 to businesses, industries, and banks. This was to enable and encourage such organizations to undertake business projects that would require the hiring of more men. Hence, unemployment would drop and people would earn money again instead of needing relief. For various reasons this didn't happen. Perhaps it was "too little and too late." Also, most of the money went to banks rather than to businesses that produced goods. Most of the latter were, perhaps rightly, afraid to think of expanding operations at that time. The RFC came under suspicion the next year when it was learned that one of the chief beneficiaries of RFC money had been a Chicago bank with which

Charles G. Dawes, Nobel Peace Prize winner and Vice President under Coolidge, had been closely allied. After serving as president of the RFC for about six months, Dawes resigned and a few weeks later the RFC loaned the Central Republic Bank of Chicago $90,000,000. In later years the government made use of the RFC to further the aims of the New Deal and, still later, for national defense. By the time it went out of business in 1956, the RFC had lent $11,000,-000,000.

Hoover also persuaded a reluctant Congress to establish a dozen Federal Home Loan Banks to enable loan associations, banks, and insurance companies to borrow money which, it was hoped, would eventually aid the homeowner who was having trouble meeting his mortgage payments. Not only had residential construction fallen almost to nothing, but also those who had homes were, in increasing numbers, finding it difficult, if not impossible, to keep up their mortgage payments. In 1932, 273,000 owners lost their homes by foreclosure and by early 1933 a thousand homeowners a day were losing their houses.

One of the most significant laws of 1932 was not proposed by Hoover and he very reluctantly signed it into law. This was the Norris-LaGuardia Act, named for its two sponsors, Senator George W. Norris and Representative Fiorello H. LaGuardia. The act for the first time gave labor unions some protection against the issuing of injunctions by the courts to restrain their activities. It also meant the end of the "yellow dog contract," whereby employers forced workmen, as a condition of employment, to agree not to join a labor union.

In the field of international relations, 1932 began on a hopeful note. In February a world disarmament conference convened at Geneva, Switzerland, under League of Nations sponsorship and with the United States and Soviet Russia participating although neither was a member of the League. The delegates debated for over a year, adjourned in March, 1933, and reconvened in October. At that time Germany, with the Nazis now in power, withdrew from the conference and resigned from the League. Democracy, fascism, and communism were more at odds than ever and any hope of disarmament was gone.

Politically 1932 was one of the most decisive in American history. After four years of Hoover's administration and three years of depression, the voters in November had a chance to render their judgment. The Republicans, for better or for worse, had no choice but to renominate Hoover and stand on his record. The Democratic nomination, however, was at the start wide open and more desirable than it had been in many years. As late June and the date for the Democratic convention neared, there were three leading candidates: Al Smith, who felt he deserved a second chance at the presidency and who had become hostile toward Franklin D. Roosevelt; John Nance Garner, of Texas, Speaker of the House of Representatives; and Roosevelt, now serving his second term as governor of New York State. By the time the convention convened, Roosevelt was clearly in the lead, thanks to the hard and astute work of his campaign manager, James A. Farley, who later became Postmaster General. At that time the Democrats required a two-thirds vote of the delegates to nominate and while Roosevelt had a clear majority on each of the first three ballots, he did not have the necessary two-thirds. Then, at the urging of his supporters, Garner withdrew in favor of Roosevelt and the latter was named on the fourth ballot, the Smith followers refusing to the end to concede defeat. Garner received the nomination for the vice presidency.

The new Democratic standard-bearer immediately began to

break tradition. He decided not to wait until later in the summer to formally accept the nomination with an air of feigned surprise, as had been the American custom for many years. Instead, with several members of his family, he flew to Chicago—in bad weather, in a trimotored, propeller-driven plane—and addressed the convention before it adjourned. "I pledge you, I pledge myself," he said, "to a new deal for the American people." The organ played the Democrats' new theme song "Happy Days Are Here Again."

Franklin Delano Roosevelt was born in 1882 into a moderately wealthy, long-established New York family of Dutch descent. After a normal education for his class and time (Groton, Harvard, Columbia Law School), he surprised family and friends by plunging into politics. As early as 1910, in what was usually a safely Republican district in his home county of Dutchess on the Hudson River, he won election to the state senate on the Democratic ticket. He attracted extra attention by doing much of his campaigning in an automobile. In the legislature he soon brought further attention to himself by siding with the reformers against the dominant Democratic machine, Tammany Hall. When Woodrow Wilson and the Democrats captured the White House in the election of 1912, Roosevelt went to Washington as Assistant Secretary of the Navy. He enjoyed the position immensely and served with distinction through World War I and until 1920. In that year, although not yet forty, he was already prominent enough to receive the vice presidential nomination. He and his running mate James M. Cox were swamped by the Republican ticket of Warren G. Harding and Calvin Coolidge, which had more appeal for the voters who wanted to return to "normalcy," as Harding put it.

The next year, while on vacation at his summer home, Roosevelt was stricken with polio and for many months it seemed that his political career was over and that he would never walk again. However, his courage and determination pulled him through. For the rest of his life he could walk only with difficulty and with the aid of heavy braces, but within three years he was back in politics. In 1924 he was active in supporting Al Smith's unsuccessful bid for the presidential nomination. Until 1928, when he ran for governor of New York for the first time, he devoted himself to a continued effort, especially at Warm Springs, Georgia, to recover further from the ravages of polio.

In 1905 Roosevelt had married Eleanor Roosevelt, a niece of President Theodore Roosevelt and his own distant cousin, as was the President also. The famous T.R. came to the wedding and at the reception attracted considerably more attention than the bride and groom. Thus began one of the most successful and useful joint careers in history. The young Eleanor had already shown an interest in social causes, but it was not until after Franklin's polio attack that she became really interested in politics. By nature shy, she learned to overcome her aversion to meeting people and speaking in public. More and more she became her handicapped husband's eyes and ears as she traveled to all parts of the country. One of the most noted of *New Yorker* cartoons is the one in which a coal miner looks up and says: "For gosh sakes, here comes Mrs. Roosevelt." After her husband became President, a Washington newspaper once ran a society page headline: "Mrs. Roosevelt Spends Night at White House." In 1933 she held the first press conference ever conducted by a president's wife and in 1935 she began a daily syndicated newspaper column called "My Day." During World War II she traveled widely abroad, and after her husband's death in 1945 she continued for more than a decade and a half to be a prominent citizen of the world, active in the United Nations and in many other causes.

Even before he received the nomination, Franklin Roosevelt had begun to surround himself with a set of advisers, many of whom differed from the usual run of advisers to politicians because they were college professors or other intellectuals. The term "Brain

Trust" was soon applied to these men, often with implications of scorn by those who were anti-Roosevelt. Raymond Moley, a Columbia University political scientist, had already helped with some of Governor Roosevelt's speeches, and he became not only the first of the academic brain trusters but also the recruiter of others. Foremost among them were Rexford Guy Tugwell and Adolf A. Berle, Jr., both also on the Columbia faculty. Tugwell, a handsome man just into his forties, was an economist with a special interest in agricultural problems. Berle, who had received his bachelor's degree from Harvard when he was only eighteen, was a specialist in corporation law and finance. Harry Hopkins, who lasted longer and came to be closer to Roosevelt than any of the academic brain trusters, was already serving under him in the administration of relief in New York State. Born in Iowa, he had become a leading professional social worker who also liked to go to the races and bet on the horses.

The brain trusters were never popular either in Washington or around the country. At best they were whipping boys for the President, pictured as a bunch of ineffectual, absent-minded professors. Sometimes, though, the same opponents who denounced them in this way also described them as extremely dangerous schemers who exercised great power. They did not, on the whole, get on very well with the practical politicians in the capital, including their fellow Democrats in Congress. The self-assurance with which they spoke and the new ideas they presented were bound to rub some people the wrong way.

The campaign, as is usual in American political life, found both candidates contradicting themselves as well as making statements and promises that were hard to justify later. Roosevelt came out for programs that would cost a good deal of money, such as more aid to the unemployed and aid to the farmer. At the same time, he promised to cut government spending by 25 per cent. Some, but by no means all, of the programs he later introduced as part of the New

Deal were foretold in his campaign speeches. Wherever he went, whatever he said, it was clear to his listeners that he was enthusiastic and confident. Roosevelt enjoyed campaigning and it showed in the lift of his chin, his big smile. Also favoring him were his family name and his long fight against illness.

Hoover, on the other hand, had never liked the rough-and-tumble game of politics. Now, having claimed credit for prosperity, he was not allowed by the people to shirk the responsibility for the depression. Street crowds booed or, at best, stood silent and sullen. By the end of the campaign he was a pathetic, beaten man. On Election Day in November the voters repudiated Hoover and his administration by an overwhelming margin. Roosevelt received 22,800,000 popular votes to Hoover's 15,750,000; 472 electoral college votes to the defeated President's 59; and carried 42 of the 48 states.

The election ended, after one term, the administration of a man who had seemed four years earlier to be just what the nation needed. He honestly believed that there was still equal opportunity for all. Government, he thought, should encourage voluntary efforts on the part of industry, labor, and other groups, but should not force action on them. He praised "rugged individualism," yet as an engineer he knew that coordination, cooperation, and planning were necessary to accomplish most things in the modern world. He did not, like some of his advisers, believe in doing absolutely nothing about the depression, but what he did, did not go far enough to do much good. In a sense he prepared the way for strong government action under Roosevelt, because by the fall of 1932 millions of people were convinced that Hoover's way would not work.

As usual, Americans in 1932 had more on their minds than politics and business conditions. The shocking news story of the year, and one that got even bigger headlines than the election, was the kidnapping of Charles A. Lindbergh, Jr., the twenty-month-old son of the national hero of the late 1920's. In 1927, at the age of twenty-five, Charles A. Lindbergh, in a single-engine plane, had made the first solo flight across the Atlantic, from New York to Paris. Acclaimed by millions as much for his modesty and boyish charm as for his achievement, Lindbergh had immediately become the nation's popular hero. He married Anne Morrow, daughter of Dwight W. Morrow, a Morgan partner and successful American ambassador to Mexico. To get away from the crowds that never let them be, the Lindberghs built a home in a remote section of New Jersey.

It was there, on March 1, 1932, that their first-born child disappeared. The newspapers and radio broadcasters had a field day, doing their best to make even more sensational the most dramatic event of the year. In spite of the effort of the police, the Federal government, and various assorted characters—some of them well-meaning, some from the underworld, some schemers and chiselers, and some crackpots—no trace of the kidnapper or the baby was found. In early April $50,000 ransom money was paid but the baby was not returned. On May 12 the body was found in woods less than six miles from the Lindbergh home. More than two years later, in September, 1934, the kidnapper was arrested, traced chiefly through the ransom money. He was Bruno Richard Hauptmann, a carpenter. He was tried and convicted in early 1935 and, after various appeals, was electrocuted on April 3, 1936, the press and radio making a Roman circus of a sad and sordid business to the end.

The Lindberghs, understandably, then withdrew further from the world. In 1936 Lindbergh, working with the scientist Alexis Carrel, helped invent a perfusion pump which could be used as an artificial heart. Lindbergh and his wife made a number of long airplane journeys together, and Mrs. Lindbergh became an author of note, with a gift for sensitive and perceptive writing, as in *North to the Orient* (1935). Later, in *The Wave of the Future* (1940), she seemed to have turned pessimistic and to be saying that the wave of the future was fascism. In the meantime her husband had been so taken by German technology and air power under the Nazis that he began to advocate what seemed to many Americans to be peace at any price. He became a leading figure in the isolationist movement. However, after the United States entered World War II, he performed valuable services for the government in his field of aeronautics.

In some areas of American life, 1932 was a year of retreat, in others, of change and innovation. Fewer than 1,500,000 automobiles were manufactured that year, about 4,000,000 fewer than three years earlier. By that year the Ford tri-motor was the leading airplane. It could carry twelve passengers at a speed of 125 miles per hour. At this time stewardesses had to be small and they had to be nurses. Amelia Earhart became the first woman to make a solo flight across the Atlantic. Five years later, when she was only forty, she disappeared in the Pacific on an around-the-world flight. Just what happened has never been determined, and in 1966 a full-length book was devoted to the subject, suggesting she may have fallen into the hands of the Japanese and been executed as a spy.

The whole field of education was hard hit by 1932. At first, schools had tried to get along by shortening the school year, by buying fewer new textbooks, and by letting teachers go. Chicago cut its teaching rolls by 1,000, and those who still had jobs were unpaid for a year or more. At one time during the depression, five out of six of the schools in Alabama were closed. As the birth rate dropped, elementary-school enrollment dropped too, but high-school enrollment went up. Many young people who would otherwise have left school for a job decided they might as well stay in school since there were no jobs. Colleges suffered as the sources of large gifts disappeared and as the income on their investments declined. Fewer students could afford college, even at the low tuition and room and board rates of those days—$1,000 would cover a year's expenses at an Ivy League college. On the other hand, no academically qualified student had any difficulty in getting into college.

On the whole, newspapers and magazines did not suffer during the depression, as far as readers were concerned. With so much news of vital personal importance and with periodical reading a relatively cheap form of entertainment, the circulation of many publications went up. There were an increasing number of mergers of newspapers, while the quantity of comics and pictures in the papers doubled between 1930 and 1940. The tabloid style and size was becoming more popular. The number of syndicated columnists grew, with so much more comment called for by the extraordinary national and international events. Walter Lippmann began his column in 1931 and soon became the most influential of those writing on public affairs, a position he held for a generation. *Newsweek* in 1933 joined the already successful *Time* as people sought news and an interpretation of its meaning. The *Reader's Digest* proved a time-killer to millions more people in the 1930's than it had before.

A best-selling book, *Life Begins at Forty,* by Walter B. Pitkin, also brought solace to many who had had the misfortune to enter the depression and middle age at the same time. More sensational, but also more related to the economic and social troubles of the times, was Erskine Caldwell's *Tobacco Road,* later made into one of the most popular plays ever to run on Broadway. James T. Farrell's *Young Lonigan,* the first part of his "Studs Lonigan" series, presented a far-from-pretty picture of modern urban life. More romantic and more widely bought was *Mutiny on the Bounty,* by James H. Hall and Charles B. Nordhoff.

Vaudeville died and was buried in 1932. The depression, the

talkies, and radio all conspired to put it out of business. In July the Palace Theater in New York, which had opened in 1913 and which had been the peak every vaudeville performer aspired to reach, closed its doors to live stage presentations. The stage's loss was radio's gain. Such stars as Eddie Cantor, Ed Wynn, Al Jolson, Fred Allen, and Jack Benny (his first sponsor was Canada Dry beverages) were soon radio headliners and had bigger audiences than ever. Comedy was emphasized on the air at a time when listeners were glad of something to take their minds off their troubles. Radio serials—"soap operas"—became popular also. "One Man's Family" went on the air in 1932 and lasted for twenty-eight years. Other popular series included "Vic and Sade," "Easy Aces," and "Rise of the Goldbergs," written and performed by Gertrude Berg. There was Uncle Don for the children, and also the Singing Lady; and the youngsters were being urged to send in box tops from what the sponsors hoped were their favorite cereals. That year NBC started an experimental television station, transmitting from the Empire State Building. Late in the year *Variety* moved its radio section into second place, right behind the movie section. Before that, radio had been in the back and vaudeville had been second.

The movies, as usual, offered something for everyone. There was *Dr. Jekyll and Mr. Hyde* and also Eugene O'Neill's *Strange Interlude.* Gary Cooper and Helen Hayes were sadly romantic in *A Farewell to Arms;* Johnny Weismuller appeared as the first Tarzan to be heard as well as seen; and *Forty-Second Street* brought back the big, gaudy musical. Technicolor was beginning to make the movies colorful. Something more than that, though, was needed to draw people into the theaters and it was in the winter of 1932–33 that two movie houses in Colorado introduced "Bank Night." This was a device of holding drawings for cash prizes and it soon spread all over the land.

On the stage Edna Ferber, one of the most popular writers of the time, was doubly represented. In the fall, after a long run, *Showboat,* the musical version of her novel, closed. At the same time the curtain went up on *Dinner at Eight,* which Miss Ferber wrote in collaboration with George S. Kaufman. In the cast were Constance Collier, Blanche Yurka, and Walter Pidgeon. A movie version the next year starred Wallace Beery and platinum blonde Jean Harlow. When the play was revived on Broadway in 1966, Miss Ferber added a few references to the depression to remind audiences of the play's original setting. For lighter entertainment in 1932 a theater-goer might have preferred *Earl Carroll's Vanities,* which boasted 155 chorus girls and a young comedian named Milton Berle.

The fad of the year was technocracy, a movement led by an eccentric engineer, Howard Scott. He and his followers first came to public notice while they were conducting an "energy survey" of North America, with headquarters at Columbia University, which seemed to give the idea intellectual status. Technocracy said that the cause of the depression was the price-and-profit system. It wanted to substitute management by scientists, technicians, and engineers, who would make the factories more productive and at the same time make sure that everyone had work and a share in the goods produced. The ordinary kind of money would be replaced by money based not on gold but on energy. In late 1932 and early 1933, technocracy was the most talked-about and written-about topic of the day. But the Technocrats quarreled among themselves, Columbia disowned them, and the vagueness and impracticality of the whole idea caused it to disappear as fast as it had arisen. The very fact that people would make so much of such a scheme was an indication of the increasingly desperate search for a way out of the depression.

In the West, this was the year the Olympic games were held in Los Angeles. In the East, it was the year Oliver Wendell Holmes, described by *The Oxford Companion to American History* as "the most distinguished of all American jurists," retired from the Supreme Court at the age of ninety-one. A junior officer in the Civil War, Holmes had been on the Supreme Court bench for thirty years, having been appointed in 1902 by President Theodore Roosevelt.

Even though Eddie Cantor sang "Now's the Time to Fall in Love" because prices were falling, the American marriage rate dropped to its lowest point in history. (The divorce rate was down, too.) No doubt about it, whether single or married, a person could live much cheaper then than now. In mid-1966 New York's *Sunday News* said: "If you're crowding middle age, you can remember when a $5 bill would feed a family for a week," and proceeded to list some 1933 prices compared with 1966: milk, 10 cents a quart then, now 27 cents; bread, 7 cents a loaf, now 18 cents; butter, 23 cents a pound, now 89 cents; eggs, then 20 cents a dozen, now 77 cents.

After the election there was a long time for the nation to wait in suspended animation politically. At that time presidents were inaugurated on March 4, not January 20, so there were four months between Roosevelt's election and his assumption of office and of power. In the meantime the White House was occupied by a man repudiated by the voters and who was unable to take any practical action. Hoover and Roosevelt met once, in late November, but the meeting accomplished nothing. Hoover still clung to the belief that the nation had been recovering until the Democratic victory destroyed confidence. Anyone could see that economic conditions were continuing to deteriorate, and the rate of bank closings around the country as Inauguration Day neared was frightening. Meanwhile Roosevelt was busy planning what his administration would do. He also, on February 15, barely escaped an assassin's bullets in Miami, Florida. Hoover's last attempt to justify himself took the form of a handwritten letter to his successor. In it he urged Roosevelt to make a statement that would reassure the country. He specified all the things Roosevelt should say and an incredulous President-elect refused when he discovered that Hoover, in effect, was urging him to repudiate all the programs and policies he had announced in his campaign.

Conditions were no better abroad. On January 30, 1933, Adolf Hitler became Chancellor of Germany even though his fanatical Nazi party did not yet hold a majority of the seats in the Reichstag. Once admitted to power—because the militarists, led by old, doddering General von Hindenburg, feared the Communists more than the Nazis—Hitler and his followers soon completed the job of intimidating their remaining opponents.

As democracy collapsed in Germany and banks failed in the United States, two of the men who were to dominate world events for the next dozen years took into their hands the fate of their peoples.

5 *The New Deal Begins*

SATURDAY, MARCH 3, 1933, was a cold, dark dreary day in Washington, D.C., matching the apprehension and despair of the people. At noon a new president would be inaugurated. Meantime the economic life of the nation was grinding to a halt as the nation's banks in state after state closed their doors lest the collapse of confidence ruin them all if depositors demanded their money.

Emotionally, if not actually, the lowest point of the depression was reached just before Franklin Delano Roosevelt became the thirty-second President of the United States. As soon as he took the oath and turned to deliver his Inaugural Address, the mood changed. In a firm, confident voice he said:

> . . . This great Nation will endure as it has endured, will revive and will prosper. So, first of all, let me assert my firm belief that the only thing we have to fear is fear itself—nameless, unreasoning, unjustified terror which paralyzes needed efforts to convert retreat into advance. . . . We do not distrust the future of essential democracy. The people of the United States have not failed. In their need they have registered a mandate that they want direct, vigorous action. . . .

This was what the people gathered in Washington and those all over the country listening to the ceremony by radio wanted to hear. In the next few days half a million of them wrote to the new President. The mood was changing even as Roosevelt reviewed the inaugural parade, an American tradition that economic collapse did not abolish. The bands, the troops, the school children, the politicians, and others marched past. The parade included a busload of veterans of the nation's Indian Wars and the most popular cowboy movie star of the era, Tom Mix, in a white suit and a big sombrero.

The mood of the country may already have been changing, but in truth there was little to cheer about that day. Many sensible people feared law and order might break down and that there would be some kind of revolution. The best estimates of the number of men and women unemployed in March, 1933, placed the total at about 12,500,000. One out of about every three wage- and salary-earners was out of a job. Nor were those with jobs getting rich. The Briggs Manufacturing Company in Detroit paid men 10 cents and women 4 cents an hour. Money income for the whole country was less than half what it had been in 1929. The index of industrial production went down from 64 to 56 (the lowest it ever reached) between December, 1932, and March, 1933. Many children had not had milk in months or years. In New York more than a fifth of the students in public schools were suffering from malnutrition.

The new President's most pressing problem was the collapse of the banking system. Since the start of the depression, more than 4,000 banks had failed and the pace was increasing. At the end of October, 1932, Nevada proclaimed a bank holiday; in February, 1933, Louisiana suspended all bank activities; and ten days later Michigan did the same. By March many other states were in a like situation. At last, on the morning of Inauguration Day, Governor Herbert H. Lehman of New York reluctantly followed suit. When the largest and richest state in the Union closed all its banks, the nation, in effect, was without banking services. In the last two weeks of Hoover's regime, depositors, losing confidence in banks, withdrew more than $1,000,000,000 and hoarded it in cash.

On March 5 Roosevelt proclaimed a four-day bank holiday, to begin the next day, and at the same time he called Congress into a special sesssion to start March 9. Besides suspending all banking functions in the entire nation, the proclamation forbade the export of gold and the redemption of currency in gold. For practical purposes, this took the country off the gold standard. On the first day that Congress convened, it was presented with the new administration's Emergency Banking Act. The House passed the bill after only forty minutes' debate; the Senate took somewhat longer, but in less than eight hours in all, the bill was signed into law by the President. The law left it to Treasury Department officials to decide which banks should be allowed to reopen and under what conditions. Half the banks, representing 90 per cent of all banking resources, were allowed to resume unrestricted operations by March 15. At the other extreme, about one bank in twenty was in such poor condition that it never did business again. In the first three weeks after banks began to reopen, more than $1,000,000,000 was redeposited in them as confidence returned.

It was not mere accident that government officials and newspapers used the euphemism "bank holiday" for the collapse of normal operations. They were frankly frightened that the public would panic if every bank in the land closed its doors. Much to the surprise of many, the American people took the bank closing in very much of a holiday spirit. There was a feeling that, bad as the situation might be, it could now get no worse and so we could start fighting our way back up. It was not unlike the feeling the day after the attack on Pearl Harbor more than eight years later. The feeling that everyone was in the same boat led, as it usually does, to more friendliness and neighborliness. A newspaper vendor might lend a banker a nickel to make a phone call. Stores extended credit. Since no one had any money to speak of, no one worried about it. The men students of Columbia College and their dates, formally dressed, held one of the school's traditional annual social events as though nothing had happened. All in all, the bank holiday was at the same time one of the most amusing and most serious episodes in American history.

The Emergency Banking Act ushered in "The Hundred Days," the period ending June 15 when the special session of Congress adjourned. In that time Congress passed fifteen major laws at the President's urging. Roosevelt, in addition, made ten speeches, held press conferences and Cabinet meetings, and made innumerable decisions concerning foreign and domestic policy. During this period many men in public life changed their minds about the new President. They had refused to take him too seriously, seeing him as somewhat of a dilettante and rather too easygoing and evasive. Now they spoke of their admiration for his determination, his drive, and his willingness to use his power and to take responsibility. The result, as Walter Lippmann wrote, was:

> At the end of February we were a congeries of disorderly panic-stricken mobs and factions. In the hundred days from March to June we became again an organized nation confident of our power to provide for our own security and to control our own destiny.

The Economy Act, the second measure of the Hundred Days, was not in keeping with most of the rest of the New Deal. It cut payments to veterans by $400,000,000 a year and the pay of Federal employees by $100,000,000. The latter's pay was restored by the end of 1933. While economy and balancing the budget restored confidence to some of the old-fashioned, conservative officials and businessmen, it cut income and spending at a time when they were most needed.

The next major law accomplished something of great personal interest to Roosevelt. It established the Civilian Conservation Corps, which had the double objective of giving unemployed young men healthful jobs and of contributing to the conservation of our natural resources. By mid-June, only two and a half months after Congress acted, the CCC had set up 1,300 camps and by August 300,000 young men were enrolled. When World War II put an end to the CCC nearly seven years later, more than 2,500,000 youths had served in it. They planted trees, built small dams, erected fire towers, fought tree diseases, and improved parks and other facilities in recreational areas. The CCC boys assisted the Forest Service in planting more than 200,000,000 trees in the Great Plains to prevent another dust bowl. All in all, the CCC was one of the most successful of the New Deal measures.

On April 19 the President announced that the country was officially going off the gold standard and on June 5 Congress backed him up. In a sense this was the most revolutionary act of the New Deal since it meant that the government was repudiating its promise to pay government bonds in gold and to give gold on demand for bills of $20 and more. The eastern bankers thought the end of the world had come. The farmers and the people of the South and West in general rejoiced. Going off the gold standard had the effect of depreciating the dollar so that it was easier to pay off mortgages and other debts incurred when the dollar had not been worth as much as hard times later made it. The move ended the drain of gold which had been flowing to Europe and it helped United States foreign trade. The abandonment of the gold standard and Roosevelt's subsequent manipulation of the value of gold and of the dollar in the autumn did not ruin the country as predicted, but neither did it accomplish as much toward recovery as the President had hoped.

The problem of relief for the unemployed and destitute had to be dealt with promptly also. Although the Federal government in 1932 had finally provided some funds to fill the gaps being left by state and municipal inability to find more money, the depression had worsened and the need was greater than ever. In May, at Roosevelt's urging, Congress set up the Federal Emergency Relief Administration with $500,000,000 to be distributed. The President drafted Harry Hopkins from New York and within two days Hopkins had organized a staff to operate FERA through the states. Because the need was so immediate and so great, much of the money had to be disbursed as direct relief, but Hopkins tried to channel as much as possible into work relief so that those receiving it would not feel they were accepting charity. For example, teachers on relief were assigned to country schools that otherwise would have had to close down.

Far more complicated to deal with but just as urgent was the farm problem. The man who had to take the lead here was the new Secretary of Agriculture, Henry A. Wallace, whose father had held the same post under President Harding. The younger Wallace was editor of an influential magazine, *Wallaces' Farmer,* and had also developed several improved strains of hybrid corn. As finally passed by Congress in May, the Agricultural Adjustment Act of 1933 was a major departure in farm policy and established principles that still apply. In brief, the law provided that the government could make agreements with farmers whereby they would promise to reduce their production of certain commodities and in return the government would pay them a subsidy. This first act covered cotton, wheat, corn, hogs, rice, tobacco, and milk. The cost of the payments was to be met by taxes on the processors of the agricultural products.

Since the crop year was too far advanced to reduce acreage by not planting as much as before, cotton farmers agreed to plow under 10,000,000 acres of their 1933 crop. In return they received about $200,000,000 in benefit payments and the price of cotton nearly doubled. Wheat did not need to be plowed under because of adverse weather conditions, but there was too much corn and too many hogs. It was therefore decided to slaughter about 6,000,000 swine, most of them, as the papers labeled them, "baby pigs." This caused a great furor. It was a terrible thing to do, many said, although they would happily have eaten the same pigs after they had grown to maturity and been slaughtered in a packing house in the normal course of events. A good many of the tears shed over the baby pigs were crocodile tears from those who opposed the New Deal program. However, the plowing under of cotton and the slaughtering of the pigs (some made into pork sausage and distributed to people on relief) again pointed up the paradox of food and clothing materials being destroyed when thousands were hungry and in need of clothes. On the other hand, no one complained louder than certain textile manufacturers when it was proposed to give surplus cotton to the needy to make their own mattresses. The AAA program did work to the extent that it raised farm commodity prices, gave the farmers greater income, and enabled them to pay their debts and stay in business. Of course, this could not be accomplished without increases in the cost of food to the consumers.

Within a week of setting up the AAA, Congress also established, in May, one of the permanent agencies of the New Deal and one that exemplified its long-range ideas rather than immediate, emergency measures. This was the Tennessee Valley Authority, a new concept in government-owned but independently operated agencies. Ever since World War I there had been an unresolved fight in Washington over what use to make of facilities developed by the government at Muscle Shoals, Alabama, during the war to produce nitrates for explosives. The leaders of the Coolidge and Harding administrations wanted to sell or lease the facilities to private industry. Advocates of public ownership of power facilities opposed this. They were led by Senator George W. Norris of Nebraska, a progressive Republican who doggedly had kept up the fight for many years.

With the approval of the Roosevelt administration, Norris drew up the measure to establish the TVA. The area involved took in parts of seven southeastern states, all of which were in the watershed of the Tennessee River and had a population of about 3,000,000. The TVA built dams, produced and sold electric power, manufactured fertilizer, controlled flood waters, showed inhabitants of the area how to end erosion of the soil, and created many attractive recreation areas. This was regional planning on a scale never before attempted in this country, and it was successful not only in erecting physical features, such as dams, but also in convincing the people of the region that it was to their own interests to join in electrification, conservation, and other activities. Today there are more than thirty multi-purpose dams in the TVA system, erected at a cost of about $900,000,000. During World War II one of the most important plants used in the development of the atomic bomb was located at Oak Ridge, Tennessee, to take advantage of TVA electric power.

In view of what had happened on the New York Stock Exchange in 1929 and what was beginning to be revealed about the shady activities that went on behind the scenes, the New Deal also quickly turned its attention to regulation of the securities market. On May 27 Congress passed the Securities Act which gave the Federal Trade Commission power to supervise the issuing of new securities. Full information about every offering had to be made public. This was the first of a number of laws that have gradually built up the present system of policing the securities market. The second important step was taken in 1934 when a separate Securities and Exchange Commission was established by law and when more restrictions were put on the free-wheeling activities of unscrupulous brokers, bankers, and promoters. Joseph P. Kennedy, father of the future President, was appointed the first chairman.

Although the previous administration had done something to help homeowners avoid foreclosure of the mortgages on their houses, the need for action was greater than ever as the real estate market and the construction industry appeared near collapse. At the President's recommendation, Congress set up the Home Owners' Loan

Corporation in June. The HOLC bought mortgages from the holders of them and rewrote them to make payment easier for the homeowner. The HOLC was enormously popular and by the time its work ended in 1936 it had made about 1,000,000 loans and refinanced $3,000,000,000 of mortgages. One out of every five mortgaged nonfarm homes in the country benefited from the HOLC.

The legislation that attempted to make the most basic change in the relation between government and the economic life of the country was the National Industrial Recovery Act, one of the last acts of the Hundred Days. The NIRA suspended the anti-trust laws through which government attempted to control the size of business and industry and to assure economic competition. It substituted a system of industrial self-government with the Federal government as arbitrator and supervisor. The law set up the National Recovery Administration which was empowered to have codes drawn up by the various industries. The codes specified maximum hours of labor, minimum wage rates, and standards of fair business practices. There was first a blanket code for all industries, and as time went on, about 500 separate codes were approved for that many industries, including the dog food industry and shoulder pad manufacturers. The cotton textile code accomplished something decades of agitation had failed to do—it abolished child labor. The blanket code set a minimum wage rate of 30 cents an hour and a maximum of 35 hours a week for factory work.

The NRA was launched with much excitement and much publicity. A somewhat stylized and fierce-looking Blue Eagle with the motto "We Do Our Part" soon became the most familiar sight in the land. All employers who signed the codes were entitled to display the Blue Eagle posters and stickers. In the larger cities lengthy parades were held, that in New York on September 12 featuring a quarter of a million marchers and a million or more spectators. There hadn't been anything like it since the Liberty Loan drives of

World War I. To administer the NRA Roosevelt appointed General Hugh S. Johnson—sometimes known as "old ironpants"— ex-soldier, ex-businessman, former member of the War Industries Board of World War I, author of stories for boys, and an irascible, energetic man determined to get things done no matter how many toes he stepped on.

One of the most important provisions of the NIRA and one that in the long run was to have more consequences than any of the rest was Section 7A, which said that employees "shall have the right to organize and bargain collectively." Employers were forbidden to interfere in such activities or to require that an employee join a company union or refrain from joining one of his own choosing. A National Labor Board was set up within the NRA to try to settle disputes, and this was the beginning of a permanent system for governmental supervision of disputes between unions and management. Many employers tried to evade the labor provisions of the NIRA while some of the unions already in existence and their leaders were slow to take advantage of the law.

One of the few who did something was John L. Lewis, president of the United Mine Workers. Beginning as a miner, he had become president of the union in 1920. An imposing figure with a mass of dark hair, he spoke in public like a frustrated actor and frequently quoted Shakespeare. His union, like all others, had been losing members steadily and had about 100,000 in 1933. By November, Lewis had brought it back to its 1920-strength of about 400,000. Also prominent on the labor scene at this time was Miss Frances Perkins, whose appointment as Secretary of Labor made her the first woman ever to serve in the Cabinet. She had begun as a social worker and had been in Roosevelt's administration in New York, serving as industrial commissioner, charged with enforcing factory and labor laws.

The NRA at first seemed to be quite a success. In March the production index had reached its lowest level, 56. By July it was up to 101 but by November it was back down to 71. Some manufacturers created a brief boom by producing as many goods as possible before the NRA codes took effect, in order to sell them at the higher prices soon to prevail. Unemployment was cut by about 2,000,000. After the codes went into effect there was a good deal of chiseling, and efforts to enforce the codes were not very successful. Big business was favored over little business; business and labor fought over unionization; the consumer was caught in the middle as some prices rose unjustifiably. NRA's goals of economic stabilization and minimum standards of working conditions were fine, but in practice it was not long before almost everyone involved was unhappy about the results.

The pro and con arguments over the NRA became academic in less than two years when, on May 27, 1935, the Supreme Court declared the National Industrial Recovery Act unconstitutional. The Court held that the law delegated powers to the President improperly and that the test case it was acting upon did not involve interstate commerce. Because the case concerned a Brooklyn poultry company and the charge that it had sold a butcher an unfit chicken, this decision of the nation's highest court has gone down in history as the "sick chicken case."

A separate section of the NIRA set up the Public Works Administration with an appropriation of $3,300,000,000. Its purpose was to stimulate the economy, not by creating jobs directly, but by contracting for the construction of many kinds of facilities that would require large quantities of materials, much machinery, and thousands of workers. To run this mammoth enterprise the President named Harold L. Ickes his Secretary of the Interior. Ickes was an old-time reformer who had been a staunch follower of Theodore Roosevelt in the Bull Moose party of 1912. Blunt, suspicious, cautious, he was known as "Honest Harold." While PWA moved slowly at first because Ickes insisted there be no waste and no graft (there was none), by the end of the decade it had completed an imposing list of projects that were permanent or near-permanent additions to the nation's basic facilities. It helped build the Hoover Dam in the West and the Triborough Bridge in New York; the port of Brownsville, Texas; the causeway connecting Florida and Key West; sewage plants; schools; hospitals with over 120,000 beds; fifty military airports; and the aircraft carriers *Yorktown* and *Enterprise* that were to have heroic records in World War II.

The last piece of legislation of the Hundred Days was the Banking Act of 1933, also known as the Glass-Steagall Act for its sponsors in Congress. At the time, its most significant section was that which separated commercial and investment banking and put restrictions on the use of bank credit for the kind of speculation that had brought the stock market crashing down four years before. Of most interest today, perhaps, is the fact that this act established the Federal Deposit Insurance Corporation, which the American Bankers Association felt sure was "unsound, unscientific, unjust and dangerous." It has turned out to be exactly the opposite.

Roosevelt's first year in office was marked by other legislative and administrative acts of importance. Federal assistance for slum clearance and public housing began through the PWA. The first public housing project in the nation began in Atlanta, Georgia, where eleven blocks of slums were torn down and replaced with new homes. Other projects followed in places such as Cleveland, Chicago, and Brooklyn. As the winter of 1933–34 approached, it became clear that more money would have to be spent on relief. To do this the Civil Works Administration was set up with the ever busy Harry Hopkins in charge. His objective was to put to work, within two months, about 4,000,000 persons and by mid-January, 1934, more than that number were on the CWA rolls. CWA was not a handout, but employed persons on relief and others in need of jobs at minimum standard wages. Because it had to get men on its rolls fast, it had to find jobs of a simple nature compared with the kind of work PWA was intended to do. The largest amount of work was done on public roads, but CWA hired 3,000 artists and writers and used their talents. It even got into archaeology by excavating prehistoric mounds for the Smithsonian Institution. In all, CWA spent about $1,000,000,000 during the winter and fulfilled well its stop-gap function.

On the lighter side of life, 1933, with the assistance of the New Deal, saw the end of prohibition, which had gone into effect in 1920. On March 13 Roosevelt urged Congress to legalize light wines and beer. In three days both houses of Congress had happily agreed, and beer with an alcoholic content of 3.2 per cent was legal and flowing freely all over the country in less than a month. The pretzel-makers could not produce their product fast enough either. In February, before Roosevelt took office, Congress had approved the Twenty-first Amendment to the Constitution, repealing the Eighteenth. On December 5, 1933, Utah was the thirty-sixth state to ratify the amendment and so it became part of the Constitution. Prohibition was dead and, subject to the laws of the various states, it was legal for Americans to drink alcoholic beverages, something many of them had been doing illegally right along.

Earlier in the year the Twentieth Amendment had been ratified. This amendment changed the date for inaugurating presidents from March 4 to January 20 and, by shifting the date when Congress was to meet each year, it ended "lame duck" sessions in which congressmen who had already been defeated at the polls could go on legislating for a few more months.

The legislation of the Hundred Days, significant as it was, brought no more change to the country than did the personality of

Franklin D. Roosevelt and his way of life. The White House, for four years almost as solemn as a tomb, was alive with a family with growing children. When a second Bonus Army invaded Washington in May, the President saw to it the men were fed, had a tent set up in which they could make all the speeches they wanted to, and encouraged Mrs. Roosevelt to pay them a friendly visit. By the nature of the times and the burst of activity in Washington, the capital became the news center of the country. Roosevelt created a good deal of this news himself by holding informal press conferences at which he charmed most of the reporters. Hoover held only 66 press conferences in four years, and all questions had to be submitted in writing. Roosevelt in his first term held 337 and was always ready to answer questions off the cuff. No president since has been able to ignore the ritual of the press conference.

It was in the use of that relatively new medium of communication, radio, that the President set a standard never surpassed for effectiveness. His talks to the nation became known as "fireside chats," and no one who ever listened to them can forget his opening phrase, "My friends." The first fireside chat was delivered on March 12, 1933, to explain the bank holiday and the steps being taken to deal with the emergency. One direct result was that people returned money to the banks. As Will Rogers said, the President took the complicated subject of banking and made even the bankers understand it. Throughout his long years in office FDR continued to make radio one of the chief tools for getting his programs accepted. He used radio to reach the people the way President Kennedy later used television.

The coming of the New Deal also marked the small beginning of a great change in the relation of the Negro to political and economic life. In proportion to the white population, twice as many Negroes were on relief, and they became grateful to the New Deal's relief funds, housing projects, and other activities that benefited them. Although he made no attempt to force integration on the South, Roosevelt ended segregation in government offices in Washington, appointed more Negroes than ever before to office, and began integration moves in the armed forces. He supported an anti-lynching bill, but refused to make it a "must" item lest it dam up in Congress other legislation he considered more vital. No civil rights bill of any kind became law during Roosevelt's twelve years, yet it was in these years that the majority of the Negroes of the country changed their allegiance, dating back to the end of the Civil War, from the Republican to the Democratic party. The obvious good will of the President and his wife were not inconsiderable factors.

In the major venture of its first year in international affairs the New Deal did not do as well as at home. The World Monetary and Economic Conference, usually called the London Economic Conference, convened in June. The nations were supposed to try to work out an agreement to stabilize currencies and to do something about reducing tariff barriers. At once a dispute broke out between the gold bloc nations, led by France, and those that had gone off the gold standard, chiefly the United States and Great Britain. The impression had gotten around that Roosevelt favored some agreement on stabilization, but when the conference met, he let it be known he would have nothing to do with it because it might interfere with his attempt to raise prices in the United States. He also disappointed the hopes of others when he decided against asking Congress to do anything about tariffs.

The ranking member of the American delegation was Cordell Hull, the new Secretary of State. Hull was an old-fashioned southern liberal who had served in the House of Representatives or the Senate most of the time since 1906. He was the author of the first Federal income tax law and a crusader for lowering the barriers that hampered international trade. The delegation as a whole was poorly chosen and badly organized. On top of that, Roosevelt suddenly and dramatically sent Raymond Moley to London in an atmosphere that led the world to expect something momentous. Instead, Moley merely presented a harmless statement in which all countries agreed they would do their best to stabilize currencies. Whereupon Roosevelt confounded even Moley by repudiating this statement and scolding all the other nations in a holier-than-thou manner. This destroyed the conference. It was not one of the President's better performances.

In the Western hemisphere Roosevelt began more auspiciously. His inaugural address had dedicated the nation "to the policy of the good neighbor" and he set out to apply it to Latin America especially, following some first moves in that direction made by the Hoover administration. At the time, the United States was looked upon by most Latin-Americans as an out-and-out imperialistic nation because of the numerous occasions on which it had intervened, both with the U.S. Marines and financial power, in their affairs. When a revolution broke out in Cuba, Roosevelt refused to intervene and the next year we gave up what had been a virtual American protectorate over Cuba ever since the Spanish-American War. In the same year the last Marines were withdrawn from Haiti and in 1936 we gave up treaty rights that had kept Panama from being really independent. At the Pan American Conference in Montevideo, Uruguay, in December, 1933, the United States agreed to join in a treaty with all the American republics which declared that no state had the right to intervene in the internal or external affairs of another. Early in 1936 Roosevelt traveled to a Pan American conference in Buenos Aires, becoming the first president to visit Latin America while in office.

The most controversial move of 1933 in foreign affairs was the formal diplomatic recognition granted the Soviet Union in November. Although the Soviets had been in power for sixteen years, America was the remaining important country that had refused to establish official relations with them. There were protests from the professional patriotic groups, but many businessmen hoped the move would open up business opportunities. Recognition of Russia turned out to be neither as fatal nor as helpful as the two viewpoints had contended.

New York City had its own kind of political new deal at the beginning of 1934. In November, 1933, short, bustling Fiorello H. LaGuardia, former progressive congressman, was elected mayor on a fusion and reform ticket that defeated the Democrats for the first time since World War I. His victory was made possible by the revelations of corruption in the administration of dapper James J. (Jimmy) Walker, who had first been elected in 1925. In September, 1932, after an investigation, Walker resigned as mayor, but New Yorkers long remembered him as typifying their city during the prohibition era. He loved the bright lights, opening nights on Broadway, the better speak-easies, and the men's styles of the late 1920's and the 1930's—the double-breasted suit, pinched in a bit at the waist, the broad lapels reaching out almost to the shoulders, and the wide neckties. LaGuardia was frumpy but honest and for three terms the best mayor the city ever had. He loved to go rushing off to fires, and when there was a newspaper strike he read the comics to the children over the radio.

In women's fashions, skirts by 1933 were down to about halfway between the knee and the ground. The natural figure had come back and the waistline was where nature had put it. Hair was still bobbed but the very short style of the flapper had given way to the more feminine shoulder-length or page-boy bob. Fingernails, which were first painted in Paris in 1929, were now being daubed with color in the United States. A revival of bicycle riding that began in 1933 helped introduce slacks for women. Men and women alike cut down drastically on their purchases of clothing during the depression even though, in January, 1934, B. Altman & Co., a leading New York City department store, offered women's spring dresses at $4.50.

In sports, the nation seemed to be moving in two directions at once. More and more people got their exercise by watching others perform, but on the other hand there was a democratization of sports, brought on in part by shorter working hours. There were more public golf courses and, while professional baseball was without question the national sport, softball became popular as a participation sport. Although professional basketball had existed since 1896, it had not made much impression. College football attracted thousands every Saturday in the fall, with many cries of "over-emphasis" from those who thought the subsidizing of students to play football and the construction of huge stadiums was not the best way to further the interests of higher education. Professional football, too, had been around for some time and in 1933 the first "world championship" game was played. The Chicago Bears won the title.

On radio the day of the dramatized and the singing commercial had already arrived. In 1933 so did "The Lone Ranger," one of the most popular programs of the era. Other favorite shows of the time were the "Eno Crime Club," "Charlie Chan," and "Death Valley Days." In the theater, twenty-seven-year-old Sidney Kingsley won the Pulitzer Prize for his play *Men in White*. Two years later he had another success in *Dead End*. Jerome Kern's *Roberta,* with its haunting and perennially popular song, "Smoke Gets in Your Eyes," was the outstanding musical show of 1933. The movies provided such diverse fare as *King Kong, The Invisible Man, Flying Down to Rio, Little Women,* and *The Three Little Pigs. King Kong* was tremendously popular, as it still is many years later no matter how many times it is shown on television. *Flying Down to Rio* brought together for the first time Fred Astaire and Ginger Rogers as a dance team that went on to still greater popularity in such movies as *The Gay Divorcée, Top Hat,* and *Swing Time.* Walt Disney's cartoon version of the three little pigs featured a tune, "Who's Afraid of the Big Bad Wolf," that was just in time to help express the nation's return of confidence in itself.

Historical novels were especially popular during the 1930's, perhaps as an escape from the frightening present, perhaps also because there were some very good ones. And some of the best were also long, giving the reader more for his money in a time when a price higher than $2.50 for a novel met with consumer resistance. The first big best seller of this type was *Anthony Adverse* by Hervey Allen, which sold more than half a million copies within two years of its publication in 1933. It was followed three years later by an even greater success. Margaret Mitchell's *Gone with the Wind,* a tremendously exciting story of the South during the Civil War and Reconstruction, won a Pulitzer Prize and sold more than a million and a half copies within a year. The movie version, which made its debut in 1939, is one of the most successful movies ever produced.

Chicago unwisely chose 1933 to open a World's Fair officially announced to celebrate "A Century of Progress" at a time when there didn't seem to be any progress. However, the fair drew 10,000,000 people and the competition for most popular exhibit was a close one between the Hall of Science and a fan dancer named Sally Rand.

The phonograph, supposedly put out of business once and for all by radio, made a comeback after 1933. The stars and the music, both popular and classical, that were heard on radio made people anxious to have them in such a form that they could listen to them whenever they wanted to. Also, recording techniques improved and electrically powered record players with changers were now available.

In spite of the depression America continued to build some of the most ambitious structures architects and engineers had ever contrived. Work was begun on Grand Coulee Dam on the Columbia River in Washington State. When it was completed in 1942 it was one of the largest dams in the world, 550 feet high and more than 4,000 feet long. In the San Francisco Bay area two mammoth bridges were begun. The Golden Gate Bridge, with its main span of 4,200 feet, became one of the most admired bridges of its type in the world. The San Francisco-Oakland Bay Bridge was a new-style, double-decked structure over eight miles long that combined two bridge spans with a tunnel.

In 1933 for the first time Americans were offered a practical way to insure themselves against the cost of hospital care through the nonprofit system that rapidly became known as Blue Cross and that before long covered millions of people.

Dance marathons also made their appearance. In these contests couples tried to see how long they could stay on their feet, more or less dancing, with only short breaks from time to time, twenty-four hours a day. The couple that held out the longest, often nearer to being unconscious than conscious but still on their feet, won the prize.

And 1933 was the year in which Albert Einstein, the world's foremost scientific genius, fled the insanity of Nazi Germany, as did many other intellectuals, to come to the United States to live and work.

6 *The New Deal at High Noon*

THE YEAR 1934, by contrast with 1933, was a quiet one for the New Deal. Far fewer major legislative measures were proposed; the sense of emergency was gone. The depression had not been ended, but conditions had improved, no doubt about that. Although there were still nearly 11,000,000 people out of work, unemployment decreased by about 1,700,000 while the number of men and women with jobs rose by almost 2,300,000. Commodity prices were up, the index of industrial production rose about six points over 1933, and stock prices gained.

Even so, the honeymoon was over for the New Deal a year after Roosevelt took office. In 1933 business leaders whose economic structure had collapsed around their ears seemed only too glad to have someone rescue them. Now that the worst was over, they recovered their self-confidence without, seemingly, learning any lessons from the crash and the depression. Although Roosevelt had resisted the temptation to nationalize the whole banking system and had, in the opinion of many competent observers, been largely responsible for preventing complete economic chaos and possible revolution, the business community showed little appreciation. Roosevelt later summed it up this way:

> In the summer of 1933, a nice old gentleman wearing a silk hat fell off the end of a pier. He was unable to swim. A friend ran down the

> pier, dived overboard and pulled him out; but the silk hat floated off with the tide. After the old gentleman had been revived, he was effusive in his thanks. He praised his friend for saving his life. Today, three years later, the old gentleman is berating his friend because the silk hat was lost.

The leaders of big business who had dominated the nation for many years did not like the rivals they saw growing up in the form of a more powerful Federal government and a more vigorous labor union movement. Although they had suffered the least in the depression, most of the rich and the powerful disliked the idea of doing anything for those who had suffered the most and who did not have a reasonable share of economic well-being. The conservatives, the bankers, the industrialists, and most of the Republicans fought any government regulation of business and opposed any taxes levied for social welfare purposes.

Most of all, they abhorred an unbalanced government budget. As noted previously, Roosevelt in the campaign of 1932 had felt impelled to come out for a balanced budget and, once in office, he made one gesture, quickly rescinded, in that direction. Obviously, the budget could not be balanced under the existing conditions. As incomes and business activity declined, tax receipts were bound to decline also—unless tax rates were raised. At the same time, if business could not put people to work so that they could eat, government would have to, both for humanitarian reasons and to prevent revolution. The Federal government had had deficits during three of the four fiscal years of the Hoover administration. Most of the deficits during Roosevelt's peacetime administration were somewhat larger than Hoover's, the largest being $3,500,000,000 in fiscal 1936. Recent criticism of the New Deal's fiscal policies has been that it did not spend enough to get business going again at a high enough level to assure full employment. Yet in 1934 Lewis Douglas, an otherwise sensible public servant, wrote the President that "conceivably the immediate fate of western civilization" hung on a balanced budget.

Conservative and business hatred of the New Deal took formal expression in the Liberty League, which was founded in August, 1934. Although the League invited all classes of people to join, it turned out to consist chiefly of conservative Democrats under the leadership of executives of such industries as Du Pont and General Motors. It formed a committee of lawyers to defend "liberty," but the committee showed interest only in cases that involved the wealthy. Former President Hoover refused to join. In spite of its noisy activities, the League had little practical influence and by its extremism may have alienated some people. Farther to the right were some Fascist groups which turned out to have even less effect on the nation and the course it took than did the Communists. Typical of the Fascists were goateed William Dudley Pelley and his Silver Shirts, obviously inspired by Hitler in Germany. While persons inclined to the left may have preferred the New Deal to the Republicans, the official Communist line was just as anti-Roosevelt as that of the Liberty League.

If Roosevelt had trouble with his opponents on the right and the left, it was nothing compared with the trouble that came to him from those who, at least part of the time, professed to be his friends and supporters and sought his endorsement of their pet panaceas for curing the depression. The most prominent of these demagogues were Huey Long, Gerald L. K. Smith, the Reverend Charles E. Coughlin, Dr. Francis E. Townsend, and Upton Sinclair.

The most powerful and the noisiest was "the Kingfish," Huey Long of Louisiana. Born on a farm, he early became the self-appointed defender of the poor people of Louisiana, a very backward state, as a path to power over the oligarchy of business, oil, and utility interests that ruled the state to their own advantage. Pudgy, red-headed, and red-faced, Long was a bundle of energy and a demagogic orator who could rouse his listeners to follow him anywhere. He could not be overlooked in a crowd, with his blustering manners and his loud clothes that featured orchid-colored shirts, pink ties, straw hats with gaudy bands, and brown and white sport shoes. In 1928, when only thirty-five, he was elected governor. At the expense of democratic government (for Louisiana soon became much like a dictator-controlled Latin-American nation) Long fulfilled many of his promises to his supporters by building highways and hospitals and providing free textbooks in the schools. He found time to establish the Sugar Bowl sports arena, too.

In 1931 he moved on to the United States Senate and for a short time both before and after the 1932 election he was a strong and effective Roosevelt supporter. His ambition and background would not let him stop there. In January, 1934, he announced his "Share Our Wealth" plan, with the slogan "Every Man a King." Long proposed to confiscate the wealth of the millionaires and distribute it so that every family had an income of at least $5,000 a year, although he never explained how this would be worked out. Every family, he said, should have a house, an automobile, and a radio. Long now had a national following and he exploited it as much as possible, frankly competing with Roosevelt for national leadership. The Democratic party feared he would run for president in 1936 on a third-party ticket and that he would poll at least several million votes. But the flamboyant rabble-rouser's star descended as fast as it had risen and in an unfortunately appropriate manner. The man who had ruthlessly crushed so many others in political warfare was shot to death in his own capitol building in Baton Rouge in September, 1935, by the son-in-law of a man whose career he had destroyed.

One of Long's henchmen, a minister named Gerald L. K. Smith, also of Louisiana, attempted to carry on the "Share Our Wealth" crusade. He was at least as efficient a rabble-rouser as Long, but he lacked Long's political power.

In the Detroit suburb of Royal Oak, from his church, the Shrine of the Little Flower, Father Coughlin had achieved a following as a radio speaker before the depression. As time went on, his interests turned more and more from religion and to politics. A furious foe of communism, he also attacked capitalism for its failure to do anything about the depression, calling it "a detriment to civilization." He had an obsession about the shortage of money and was especially eager to put silver on an equal footing with gold as a way of ending the depression. By 1934 Father Coughlin was receiving more mail than the President and probably had the largest regular listening audience in the world. He also had voluntary contributions of about half a million dollars a year pouring in.

At first Father Coughlin supported Roosevelt, but as time went on he began to denounce him because he did not move fast enough in doing things the way Father Coughlin thought they should be done. In November he announced the founding of the National Union for Social Justice, which advocated the nationalization of banks, utilities, and natural resources. Father Coughlin became increasingly anti-Semitic and pro-Fascist and eventually he was silenced by his superiors in the Roman Catholic Church.

On no group was the depression harder than on retired, elderly men and women. Only about half the states had old age pensions of any kind and the sums granted seldom exceeded $15 a month. A Long Beach, California, physician, himself in his mid-sixties, who saw all around him the distress of the older generation, resolved to do something. He was Dr. Francis E. Townsend and in January, 1934, he announced the formation of Old Age Revolving Pensions, Limited. Under the plan every retired person over sixty would receive from the government $200 a month, provided he spent all of the money within thirty days. Townsend proposed a 2 per cent tax on business transactions to finance the scheme. In spite of its unsound economics the plan, aided by professional promoters, caught on like wildfire among the elderly. It had elements of a religious revival, appealing as it did primarily to Americans who grew up in a more rural nation and who were distressed almost as much by modern fashions and morals and the urbanization of the country as by economic hardship. Townsend claimed 25,000,000 persons signed his petitions, but a bill to establish the plan was defeated in Congress.

In 1936 a temporary alliance of Smith, Father Coughlin, and Dr. Townsend sought to capture the White House by founding the Union party. They nominated William Lemke, a North Dakota congressman, for the presidency, but the combined political strength of these masters of demagoguery turned out to be pathetically small. Lemke polled only 892,000 votes.

Rather different from such men was Upton Sinclair, long a utopian Socialist and a prolific author of novels. With the aid of one of his novels, *I, Governor of California, and How I Ended Poverty,* he captured the Democratic nomination for governor in that state in 1934. His platform was summed up in "End Poverty in California," which translated neatly into EPIC. Although Roosevelt rather liked Sinclair, he did not think it expedient to give him much support. Sinclair frightened the business interests with his proposals for reorganizing society in cooperative nonprofit groups. With the assistance of professional public relations consultants, here used in a political campaign for the first time, the Republicans defeated Sinclair's bid for utopia on the West Coast.

In the area of legislation, one of the most important acts of 1934 marked a turning-away from economic nationalism and an attempt to increase American foreign trade by lowering tariff barriers. Between 1929 and 1932 the total foreign trade of the United States had dropped from about $9,600,000,000 to slightly less than $3,000,000,000. There was some increase after that as business conditions picked up. Secretary of State Hull, who had something of an obsession about freer international trade, prevailed on the President to propose a reciprocal trade agreements act to Congress. The bill became law after a difficult struggle in Congress because it took some power away from the legislators and gave it to the chief executive. Under the law the President could reduce American tariff rates up to 50 per cent, provided other countries made similar concessions. Agreements were reached with seventeen different countries, and the law has been renewed with various modifications ever since its original three-year term. While reciprocity did not accomplish as much as Secretary Hull claimed it would, it did more to encourage trading among nations than anything the United States had done in many years.

In a new and rapidly growing field, Congress and the President established the Federal Communications Commission as successor to the Federal Radio Commission of 1927. Its chief concern was with radio broadcasting, in which field it was given the power to license stations, assign frequencies, and prescribe the nature of the services stations should perform.

In November the voters had their first chance to pass judgment on the New Deal. While the Democrats from Roosevelt on down were confident, they rather expected to lose some seats in Congress (since the party in power usually does at midterm elections). To almost everyone's surprise the Democrats gained instead of lost. The Republicans lost seats in the House so that the Democrats had 318 members to the Republicans' 104, with Progressives and Farmer-Laborites making up the balance. In the Senate there were 9 new Democratic senators and the balance was 69 to 27. In both houses the Republicans had never had so small a part of the total. One of the new Democratic senators was Harry S. Truman of Missouri.

Victory in the election made Roosevelt's position more difficult rather than easier. On the right, the conservative Republicans that remained in office were utterly opposed to him, although they offered no constructive program of their own. On the left, the new Congress meant more pressure on the President for extreme measures such as those of Senator Long and Dr. Townsend. Roosevelt himself seemed for a while to be uncertain as to what course he should now pursue, but gradually a new program unfolded. It emphasized reform rather than recovery and made no further attempt to reach a position of consensus where business and labor, right and left, could meet. This was how the second New Deal began.

One of the two most important pieces of domestic legislation of 1935 was not launched by the White House. This was the National Labor Relations Act, or the Wagner Act, as it became known because of its sponsor, Senator Robert F. Wagner of New York, father of a future mayor of New York City. Although the bill was introduced into Congress in February, it was not until May that Roosevelt announced his support. The bill became law on July 5. The NLRA turned the employer-versus-union situation completely around. Now the weight of the government was behind labor instead of industry. Employers were required to bargain with their employees and a number of "unfair labor practices" were specified in which employers could not indulge. A National Labor Relations Board was established, with power to hold elections to determine which union should represent the workers in a plant or industry. The NLRB, however, was not a mediation service and had no power over the actual terms of a labor contract. A number of high-priced lawyers, on behalf of the Liberty League, at once took it upon themselves to declare the law unconstitutional. This encouraged industry to defy the law until, in April, 1937, the Supreme Court upheld its constitutionality. Over the years, while the NLRA has remained the basis of employer-employee relations, it has been modified, especially by the Taft-Hartley Labor Act of 1947, which sought to redress the balance between the two sides.

Two years earlier, under the impetus of Section 7A of the NIRA, organized labor had begun to stir. The bitter opposition of industry to union organizing led to a number of strikes. The spring and summer of 1934 saw more strikes than for two decades, including one in the automobile industry, a nationwide textile strike, and a general strike in San Francisco. They were not successful and many labor leaders felt the President was not on their side because he attempted to prevent or end some strikes in ways that resulted in the unions getting little benefit. Nevertheless, between 1933 and 1935 union membership increased by about 1,000,000.

Now, with the Wagner Act, organized labor had another and better chance. One group of labor leaders soon felt that the old-time, craft union leadership of the American Federation of Labor was dragging its feet and not taking advantage of the situation. In October, John L. Lewis, with such chief lieutenants as Philip Murray, Sidney Hillman, David Dubinsky, and Walter P. Reuther, formed within the AFL the Committee for Industrial Organization. Its purpose was to organize into industrial unions the workers in the mass-production industries, particularly automobiles, steel, textiles, and utilities. In less than two years the CIO had achieved its hardest goals: unions had been recognized in steel and autos, the two large industries that had been determined never to bargain with labor. In achieving this, the CIO developed new methods, the most spectacular of which was the sit-in strike. First used in the rubber industry in 1936, it received the most publicity early in 1937 when auto workers at the Flint plant of General Motors refused to leave the building. In March, 1937, the clerks in a Woolworth store on Fourteenth Street in New York City staged a sit-in strike to demand wages of $20 a week. The technique could not be used for long, however, because the Supreme Court declared it illegal. In the fall of 1937 the AFL expelled the CIO unions from its ranks and the next year the CIO changed its name slightly to the Congress of Industrial Organizations. By that time it claimed 4,000,000 members. Nearly two decades later, in 1955, the two major sections of the American labor movement reunited as the AFL-CIO.

The President had indicated that he favored social welfare legislation, but again his hand was forced by pressures from Congress and elsewhere. In 1934 he set up a committee to study the problem; in January, 1935, he sent a message to Congress and an administration bill was introduced; in August it became law. Until its passage the United States for many years had lagged behind a number of other nations, especially those of western Europe, in providing protection for its citizens against the economic vicissitudes of life. The Social Security Act provided several kinds of assistance. Best known is the old age annuity system, which is the only part administered directly from Washington. Employer and employee were both to contribute to old age, survivors, and disability insurance by payroll taxes, and persons became eligible for pensions at the age of sixty-five. The minimum was set at $10 a month and the maximum at $85. Over the years the minimum and maximum amounts paid and the number of people covered have increased considerably but the basis is the same. The act also set up, through the states, an unemployment insurance system. In addition, there were provisions for aid to the needy elderly, blind persons, and crippled and neglected children. Despite criticisms from both conservatives and liberals, the act began to operate smoothly and was the New Deal law that in the long run affected the lives of more people than any other.

The other measures of 1935 were aimed at reforming evils the New Dealers felt the stock market crash and subsequent revelations of fancy manipulations in high finance had spotlighted. The Public Utility Holding Company Bill was passed after a bitter fight in which lobbyists for the power companies spent at least $1,000,000 and resorted to some rather shady practices. It attempted to remove some of the layers of holding companies that had been used to combine operating companies for the greater profit of the insiders. An outstanding example held before the public was the collapse of Insull's empire. The President also proposed revisions of the income tax laws to put a heavier burden on wealthy individuals and corporations and thus redistribute some of the wealth of the nation. By the time it became law, however, it had been watered down considerably. It did provide for a graduated corporation income tax that favored small businesses and it did increase estate taxes, tax rates on large incomes, and levy an excess profits tax. Whereas in 1933 the NRA concept had favored bigness in business, these two laws implied a return to the older concept that all bigness in business was bad and that efforts should be made to keep business units small.

Of considerable significance in the long run was the Rural Electrification Administration which the President established in May, 1935. Private power companies had shown no interest in providing electric service to most of the nation's farms because they did not think it would be profitable. The REA was empowered to loan money to establish such rural electric service. When the REA began, only about one out of every ten farms enjoyed electric service; by 1941 four out of ten farms had it; and by 1950, nine out of ten. The Resettlement Administration, which was succeeded in 1937 by the Farm Security Administration, attempted to improve the lot of the poorer farmers, the tenant farmers, and the sharecroppers, by making it possible for them to move to better land. The new agricultural policy as expressed in the AAA had actually worked to the detriment of these groups. The AAA benefits did not trickle down from the landowner to the tenant farmer, and the large landowners found it was more profitable to move such people off the land in order to combine farms into larger areas and use the latest machinery. This was known as being "tractored off" the land. The RA was able to resettle only 4,441 families; the FSA was more successful but did not solve the problem of rural poverty.

The New Deal had to continue relief measures of various kinds in 1935 and in the process introduced an innovation or two. The Federal government now concerned itself with work relief and returned the rest of the relief problem to the states and localities. Out of the Emergency Relief Appropriation Act of nearly $5,000,000,000, the President established the Work Progress Administration under Harry Hopkins. Again Hopkins set out to create as many jobs as fast as possible and by 1941 WPA had employed 8,000,000 different individuals. With labor that was for the most part unskilled, WPA built or improved schools, hospitals, and playgrounds. It even constructed a ski lodge on top of Mount Hood in Oregon. There were charges of loafing and of useless and inefficient work, but on the whole the country got more for its money than pessimists expected.

An innovation of the WPA was the use of the professional skills of writers, artists, musicians, and theatrical people in ways that would enrich the nation culturally. The Federal Writers' Project, for example, aided over 6,000 unemployed journalists, novelists, and poets between 1935 and 1939. Among them were authors who became well known later, such as John Cheever, Richard Wright (who did a WPA guide to Harlem), and Nelson Algren (who before joining the WPA project had been living on an advance of $30 a month from his publisher while he worked on a novel). The Writers' Project turned out 378 books and pamphlets that were published through commercial publishers. These works included 51 state and territorial guides, many of which are still in print.

The Federal Art Project, in similar vein, gave artists a chance to decorate many post offices and other public buildings with murals. It employed such artists as Willem de Kooning and Jackson Pollock. In addition to the WPA impetus, there were interesting stirrings in American art during this period. The depression turned many painters away from conventional art subjects and pointed them toward a rediscovery of America—coupled very often with paintings that criticized the social system. There were regionalists, such as

Thomas Hart Benton, the best-known muralist; John Steuart Curry, whose *Baptism in Kansas* is typical of his work; and Grant Wood, famous for *American Gothic.* Among the social critics were Charles Burchfield, Edward Hopper, William Gropper, and Reginald Marsh. Artists of this kind portrayed strikes, soil erosion, self-serving politicians, ugly architecture, and the horrors of unemployment rather than still lifes or upper-class children.

The Federal Theatre Project not only gave employment to many actors, directors, and stage designers, but also brought live theater to many persons who had never seen it before. It experimented with such productions as *Macbeth,* done in a modern setting with a Haitian background. It produced T. S. Eliot's new play, *Murder in the Cathedral,* and two very successful modernizations of Gilbert and Sullivan, with Negro casts, called *The Hot Mikado* and *The Swing Mikado.* The Federal Theatre Project also pioneered dramatizations of current economic and political problems in productions such as *Triple A Plowed Under* and Sinclair Lewis' *It Can't Happen Here.* Finally, it gave impetus to other experiments in the writing and producing of plays. A number of contemporary dramas of social significance were presented in the 1930's by the Group Theatre, which had been founded in 1931. The Group's best-known playwright was Clifford Odets, whose first success was *Waiting for Lefty,* produced in 1935 when the author was only twenty-nine. The play concerned a taxi drivers' strike and was staunchly pro-labor union. Another young playwright typical of the period was Marc Blitzstein, whose experimental play, *The Cradle Will Rock,* staged in 1937, depicted the social injustices of the day. Maxwell Anderson, whose first play was produced in 1923, ten years later received the Pulitzer Prize for *Both Your Houses,* a satire on congressional corruption. He became in the 1930's the leading exponent of drama in poetic form with such plays as *Winterset* (1935), which was suggested by the Sacco-Vanzetti murder case, and *High Tor* (1936), a fantasy on the theme of individualism versus modern industrialism.

The Federal Music Project was a godsend to professional musicians, thousands of whom had been thrown out of work by the talkies and radio as well as by the depression. It is estimated that they gave 150,000 programs, heard by over 100,000,000 people. In addition, half a million students got free music lessons. The project did much to make known the music of American composers such as Aaron Copland and Virgil Thomson. Gradually Congress restricted the activities of these projects in the arts because many writers, stage producers, and artists had a strong tendency to criticize the status quo.

Another innovation that was popular with young people and helped make it possible for many of them to continue going to school was the National Youth Administration. In seven years it gave part-time employment to more than 600,000 college students, over 1,500,000 high-school students, and 2,600,000 jobless youths not in school. High-school students could earn no more than $6 a month and university graduate students no more than $30, but in those days such sums were welcome and useful. From 1935 to 1937 the state director of the NYA in Texas was young Lyndon B. Johnson, who left the job because he got himself elected to Congress.

Events of 1935 showed that the spirit of isolationism was getting stronger in the United States. The nation's revulsion against its World War I crusading spirit seemed to many to be justified by the failure of our allies to pay their war debts and, more recently, by Hitler's rise to power in Germany. In 1934 a Senate investigating committee headed by Senator Gerald P. Nye began to probe into the actions of bankers and munitions-makers during World War I. Evidence of exceedingly high profits was revealed and there were many bitter references to "merchants of death," but there was never any indication that their actions had played any significant part in securing America's entry into the war. Nevertheless, the dominant opinion was that the United States could stay out of any future war if it had nothing to do with other nations in the way of treaties or in the exporting of armaments. At the end of August Congress passed the Neutrality Act of 1935, which forbade the shipment of arms to belligerents, barred loans or credits to them, and prohibited American vessels from carrying war materials to nations that were at war. Roosevelt signed the bill, although he did not really agree with it, most of all because it did not distinguish between aggressor and victim.

It was not long before the Neutrality Act had to be invoked. In October Italy, under the leadership of its dictator Benito Mussolini, invaded Ethiopia on the flimsiest of excuses. The President promptly invoked the new law, which pleased the isolationists, but he was hoping that this would encourage the League of Nations to invoke sanctions against Italy. Nothing effective was done by the League, however, and the League's seemingly cynical attempt to arrange a deal with Italy merely confirmed the American isolationists in their suspicion of the low moral quality of European nations.

In central Europe, meanwhile, Hitler was keeping international affairs in as much of a turmoil as possible. In July, 1934, Chancellor Engelbert Dollfuss of Austria was assassinated by native Nazis, although they failed in their bid to seize the state. On August 2 aged President von Hindenburg died and Hitler, combining the offices of chancellor and president, proclaimed himself Führer of the Reich. On March 10, 1935, Hitler formally and unilaterally denounced the Versailles Treaty. A brighter, although premature, note was struck in 1934 when the American Congress voted to give the Philippine Islands their independence on March 12, 1945. Because of World War II it became necessary to postpone this event until July 4, 1946.

Nature turned on the farmers of the Great Plains area of the West in the midst of their other troubles. This semi-arid territory had been overgrazed by cattle; then, when World War I increased the demand for food, it was turned into farm land. Man got away with this during the 1920's because there was enough rainfall, but the 1930's added drought to economic affliction. The crops dried up, the land turned to dust. Beginning in the late fall of 1933 enormous dust storms began to blow from west to east, the first ones turning the Dakota skies into a "black blizzard." The skies were darkened as far east as Albany, New York. In the spring of 1934 the dust storms, from Texas to Canada, blew eastward. The dry soil drifted like snow; automobiles had to use their headlights at noon; families stuffed door and window cracks to keep from being choked; livestock died of thirst; and the dust blew farther east and fell into the Atlantic Ocean. Millions of acres of farm land lost their topsoil and thousands of families fled their homes.

Most of them headed for California, in battered trucks and limping passenger cars, with such furniture and other possessions as they could stuff inside or fasten to the sides and roof. Although they came from a dozen states, they were known mostly as "Okies," since Oklahoma was especially hard hit. The chronicler of their odyssey was John Steinbeck, later to receive the Nobel Prize in literature. *The Grapes of Wrath,* published in 1939, was the novel of the decade that best represents the depression years. As Steinbeck described the dust bowl:

> The air and the sky darkened and through them the sun shone redly, and there was a raw sting in the air. During a night the wind raced faster over the land, dug cunningly among the rootlets of the corn, and the corn fought the wind with its weakened leaves. . . . The dawn came, but no day. In the gray sky a red sun appeared, a dim red circle that gave a little light, like dusk; and as that day advanced, the dusk slipped back toward darkness, and the wind cried and whimpered over the fallen corn. . . . When the night came again it was black night, for the stars could not pierce the dust to get down, and the window lights could not even spread beyond their own yards.

In quite another area of American life there were also spectacular events in the 1930's. Although the depression itself seemed to have caused surprisingly little crime, the gangsters and racketeers bred by the prohibition era turned to other illegal activities, including kidnapping and bank holdups. When state and local authorities appeared unable to cope with the more daring criminal exploits, the Federal Bureau of Investigation, which had been headed by J. Edgar Hoover since 1924, stepped in. Congress obliged by making various crimes Federal offenses in one way or another. The classic story of the G-men and the one that first made them front-page news was the saga of John Dillinger. Dillinger was a proficient bank robber who could, and did, get out of almost any jail. Then the G-men moved in, labeled Dillinger "Public Enemy Number One," and started to track him down. He got away from them twice, but in July, 1934, they shot him dead as he came out of a movie theater in Chicago. Before the year was out the FBI agents had shot down two more public enemies, Pretty Boy Floyd and Baby Face Nelson. Soon there were movies and radio serials about the G-men, and small boys became Junior G-men instead of cowboys.

Despite the depression, medical science went on quietly making new discoveries. Sulfanilamide was pioneered in Germany in 1935 and before long it and other of the sulfa drugs were in daily use. The iron lung, for those with paralyzed chest muscles, especially from polio which was then a dread disease among children, was invented in 1930. There was no vaccine against polio and during the decade the number of cases per year in the United States went as high as about 30,000 although the average was lower. Whooping cough, which has now about disappeared, reached its maximum in the mid-thirties with a peak year of more than 250,000 cases. Diphtheria was already beginning to disappear, the number of cases per year declining steadily in the 1930's from a peak of more than 60,000 to about

15,000. By 1940 anti-typhus vaccine was in production and dessicated blood plasma was being used regularly.

In transportation the depression years turned out to be the period when the largest ocean liners ever built were launched. They were led by the French ship *Normandie* in 1935, which was 981 feet long. The next year the British superliner *Queen Mary* made her maiden voyage. She was 975 feet long. In 1940 her sister ship, the *Queen Elizabeth,* became the largest of them all, 987 feet long and with a gross tonnage of 83,673. In 1938 the *Queen Mary* set a new record for Atlantic crossings by making the trip in three days, twenty hours, and forty-two minutes. A major sea tragedy occurred in the summer of 1934 when the liner *Morro Castle* caught fire off the New Jersey coast under mysterious circumstances. By the time the ship drifted onto the beach 135 lives were lost.

Airmail service across the Pacific Ocean began in 1934 and three years later passengers began to be carried also. The planes used were the China Clippers, which were flying boats, landing on and taking off from the water rather than land. The first trans-Atlantic air service for both passengers and mail started operating in 1939. In the automobile field, 1934 was the year streamlining, as the car manufacturers then understood it, was introduced by Chrysler with its "airflow" design. The sloping front end was not accepted by the public at once, but this was the end of angularity in autos.

One of the authors of 1934 was Herbert Hoover, whose *The Challenge to Liberty* was a straightforward presentation of his political position. In fiction 1934 was marked by F. Scott Fitzgerald's *Tender Is the Night*; in poetry by Edna St. Vincent Millay's *Wine from These Grapes*; on the stage by Lillian Hellman's *The Children's Hour*. The next year Sinclair Lewis used the novel form to warn of fascism in America in *It Can't Happen Here;* Robert Sherwood's *The Petrified Forest* appeared on the stage. In 1935 Helen Hayes opened in *Victoria Regina,* which ran for 517 performances on Broadway and brought Miss Hayes recognition as a first-class actress. Vincent Price played opposite Miss Hayes as young Prince Albert.

The years 1934 and 1935 continued to be fine ones for movie-goers. *Of Human Bondage* made a star of Bette Davis; the best comedy of 1934 was *It Happened One Night,* with Clark Gable and Claudette Colbert; *The Thin Man,* with suave William Powell and sleek Myrna Loy, treated a mysterious murder in a sophisticated way; and Donald Duck made his first appearance on the screen. The next year movie-goers saw noble Ronald Colman in *A Tale of Two Cities* and W. C. Fields as Mr. Micawber in another Dickens epic, *David Copperfield. The Private Life of Henry VIII* in 1935 was the first British-made film to be a hit in the United States, while British stories seemed to provide much good subject matter for the screen, as witness: *The Barretts of Wimpole Street; Berkeley Square; The Lives of a Bengal Lancer;* and *Becky Sharp,* the first feature-length movie in full color.

The public continued to find escape in sports, too, with professional boxing and baseball attracting the most attention. In 1934 the incomparable Babe Ruth ended his career with the New York Yankees, having joined them in 1920. His lifetime record of 714 home runs has never been equaled. The Babe was easily the highest paid player of his day and for two seasons received around $80,000 a year—this in the midst of the depression and with low income tax rates. When a friend asked him if he didn't think his salary was rather high considering that he was getting more than President Hoover, the Babe is supposed to have replied: "Yeah, but I had a better season than he did." The first night baseball game in the major leagues was played in Cincinnati in 1935. That same year an amateur sport among college boys was goldfish-swallowing.

In the early years of the decade popular music was typified by such slow and lovely tunes as Hoagy Carmichael's "Star Dust," the hit of 1932; "Night and Day," the same year; and "Stormy Weather," in 1933. Authentic jazz never died out, though, and about 1934 it began to be popular and fashionable as "hot jazz" and "swing." Perhaps the somewhat better times of the early New Deal made people feel more receptive to the peppier spirit of jazz. In 1934 a little-known clarinetist named Benny Goodman formed his own band and began to make swing popular on a radio program, "Let's Dance." By 1935 the swing era was in full bloom and Goodman was well on his way to becoming the "King of Swing." Count Basie organized his own band that year and he, too, was soon one of the leaders, after an early engagement in Kansas City where the players got $18 a week and Basie $21. Soon the hepcats and the jitterbugs were in the groove and in the next few years the favorite dances bore such names as the Big Apple, the Shag, and the Lindy Hop. The scenes of mad enthusiasm when Goodman and his band played at New York's Paramount Theater were comparable with those caused by the Beatles when they appeared in America a generation later and were mobbed by the sons and daughters of Goodman's fans.

Chain letters were the most popular get-rich-quick scheme of 1934. When you received a letter with ten names listed, you sent a dime to the name on the top, added your name at the bottom, and sent the letter to ten of your friends. If no one broke the chain and if everyone kept on sending the list to ten friends, each of whom sent it to ten friends, obviously everyone would get rich. But somehow no one ever did. A more innocent pastime, popular in 1935, was "handies." You made some kinds of motions with your hands and got friends to try to guess what they represented. For example, if you held one hand directly above the other, all fingers extended, up in one case and down in the other, and wiggled all the fingers, that represented five men taking a shower. Judging by newspaper space devoted to it and the way people talked about it, the most sensational event of 1934 was the birth on May 28 of quintuplets—five little girls—to Mrs. Oliva Dionne in a backwoods Canadian village. The quints soon became Canada's prime tourist attraction and the babies were made wards of the King of England to prevent undue commercial exploitation of them. Color film came into ordinary use in 1935 and that year, too, air conditioning did a business totaling $17,500,000, a far cry from what was ahead, but it was in the 1930's that the small window unit was developed. And in "Middletown," which was really Muncie, Indiana, repeal and better times prompted a local hotel to open a night club. There was a cover charge of 55 cents on Saturday and Sunday nights.

The whole nation was saddened in August, 1935, when the genial comedian with the pointed comments on America and Americans, Will Rogers, was killed in an airplane crash in Alaska. At the time, Rogers, who had first made a hit back in 1915 in the *Ziegfeld Follies,* was flying with Wiley Post. Post, who had set an around-the-world record with Harold Gatty in 1931, had two years later become the first person to fly around the world alone. Rogers left behind his summary of the United States and the depression. We were, he said, "the only nation in history that ever went to the poorhouse in an automobile."

7 *Triumph and Trouble*

WITH THE EXCEPTION of a spectacular election victory, the years 1936 and 1937 were not successful ones for Franklin Roosevelt and the New Deal, either at home or abroad, in legislation or in the economic situation.

At home the New Deal was having more trouble with the Supreme Court than with the Republicans. The Court, as has been noted, had already struck down the National Industrial Recovery Act, and by the end of 1935 it had also declared unconstitutional the Railroad Retirement Act and the Frazier-Lemke Farm Mortgage Act. In early January, 1936, by a 6 to 3 decision, the Court decided that the processing tax levied as part of the Agricultural Adjustment Act was unconstitutional because it expropriated money from one group for the benefit of another. This destroyed another major program of the New Deal. The court decision made it necessary for the government to return to the processors of agricultural products about $200,000,000 in taxes they had paid—and which they had undoubtedly already passed on to their customers in the form of higher prices.

Within two months the President and Congress passed a new law to replace the AAA. This one was based on conservation. It paid benefits to farmers for planting soil-enriching crops and grasses instead of the usual commercial crops which depleted the soil. The same ends were accomplished as previously, but there was more emphasis on conservation rather than on crop reduction alone. It was somewhat of a stop-gap measure and in 1938 a new Agricultural Adjustment Act became law—and two years later was found constitutional by the Supreme Court. The new law established the idea of the "ever normal granary." In years when crops were large, the AAA could make loans to farmers and store the crops for sale in years of low yield. This system, it was hoped, would keep the prices of farm products stable. Farmers could, by a two-thirds vote, fix the acreage to be planted in staple crops and set marketing quotas. Soil conservation measures were also continued.

The particular problem of farm policy was solved but the Supreme Court was considering the constitutionality of other measures. In May, 1936, it voided the labor provisions of the Bituminous Coal Conservation Act; the same month it declared invalid the Municipal Bankruptcy Act. On June 1, it threw out a New York State minimum wage law in such a way as to imply that neither the states nor the Federal government could pass such laws.

In 1935, when the NIRA had been nullified by the Court, Roosevelt had held a press conference at which he had discoursed for almost an hour and a half on the decision and its meaning. Naturally he was strongly at odds with the Court, but he restrained his temper and threatened no particular action. It was on this occasion that he described the decision as a "horse-and-buggy definition of interstate commerce," and the "horse-and-buggy" part of the sentence was soon applied directly to the Court and its members by New Deal sympathizers. Now, in mid-1936, the President continued his self-restraint and did not indicate what, if anything, he proposed to do. At the moment there was a presidential election he had to attend to.

Roosevelt was certain to be nominated for a second term by the Democrats. The convention at Philadelphia was therefore a rather dull affair until the President appeared on June 27 to deliver his acceptance speech. In it he used two phrases that have been associated with his name ever since. In a major part of the talk he bluntly attacked the "economic royalists," the business leaders whose cooperation he had once hoped for. He said of them:

> The royalists of the economic order have conceded that political freedom was the business of the government, but they have maintained that economic slavery was nobody's business. . . . These economic royalists complain that we seek to overthrow the institutions of America. What they really complain of is that we seek to take away their power.

And near the end of the speech, he declared:

> There is a mysterious cycle in human events. To some generations much is given. Of other generations much is expected. This generation of Americans has a rendezvous with destiny.

The Republicans had met earlier in Cleveland and they had more of a problem of selecting a candidate. Former President Hoover obviously wanted the nomination in order to have a chance to vindicate himself. And during the convention, his biting attack on the New Deal brought the delegates to their feet with wild enthusiasm, but the nomination went to Alfred M. Landon, governor of Kansas. Landon had been built up as the "Kansas Coolidge," who had balanced the budget of his state while the New Deal was spending recklessly. Landon's opponents said he had been able to balance his budget only because of the Federal money he received through the New Deal. In any event, he was not a die-hard conservative, as some tried to picture him. He was more in the progressive tradition and had been a supporter of Theodore Roosevelt in his Bull Moose campaign of 1912.

While Republican orators spent much time proclaiming that the re-election of Roosevelt meant the end of the "American way of life," their platform did not differ greatly from that of the Democrats. In an attempt to capture the middle-of-the-road vote, the Republicans asserted they could manage the New Deal better than the Democrats. William Randolph Hearst, the newspaper publisher who had originally supported Roosevelt, was one of the first backers of Landon. The great majority of newspapers opposed Roosevelt. Al Smith "took a walk" from the party he had led so honorably in New York State, and announced he was for Landon. New Deal haters who also disliked the new rage in popular music, swing, blamed it on Roosevelt. He was criticized because the Surgeon General of the United States used the then-taboo word syphilis over the radio. A full-page Peter Arno cartoon in *The New Yorker* had the leader of one group of obviously well-to-do citizens calling to another: "Come along. We're going to the Trans-Lux [a newsreel theater] to hiss Roosevelt." In another cartoon one of Helen Hokinson's cautious suburban dowagers remarked: "Of course, we must draw some sort of distinction between wishing to overthrow the government and not liking the present administration."

The campaign itself was carried on by the two candidates in a combination of old and new methods. Radio was now the most important medium for reaching the masses of the voters with important speeches, but the traditional campaign trains rumbled endlessly over the railroads so that the candidates could be seen in person. It was a grueling experience, what with speeches in the middle of the night, the dirt and the noise, newspapermen frantically writing their stories, and local politicians by the score swarming on and off the train. Roosevelt, as usual, prospered from campaigning, and his open, enthusiastic personality gave him a great advantage over the affable but quiet Landon.

When Election Day came and the votes were counted, it appeared that, as someone remarked, everyone was against Roosevelt except the voters. He carried every state except Maine and Vermont (as Postmaster General Farley had predicted) ; his popular vote was 27,752,309 to Landon's 16,682,524; he had 523 electoral votes to Landon's 8. In addition, the Democrats gained in the House and in the Senate so that their top-heavy majorities were 330 to 90 and 76 to 16, respectively.

The 1936 election not only finished Landon's political career and set the Republican Party back on its heels for another sixteen years, it was also the final blow to one of the nation's leading magazines, the *Literary Digest.* According to the *Digest*'s straw poll, which in the past had been right, Landon would easily win the election. However, the *Digest* collected most of its straw votes from automobile owners and those who had telephones. In those days this was hardly a scientific cross-section of the population. Dr. George Gallup, who had been in the polling business only about a year, predicted Roosevelt would win, but not by as much as his actual triumph. The day of the more-or-less scientific public opinion poll had arrived; the day of the *Literary Digest* was over. In February, 1938, it ended publication and its subscription list was purchased by *Time,* a newer kind of news magazine that was making the *Digest* obsolete anyway.

On January 20, 1937, Franklin D. Roosevelt took the oath of office as President of the United States for the second time. The man who administered the oath was Charles Evans Hughes, dignified, bewhiskered, the very image of a chief justice of the United States.

Hughes had been appointed chief justice in 1930 by President Hoover. With Owen J. Roberts, also a Hoover appointee, Hughes represented a middle position. Definitely in the conservative camp were Willis Van Devanter, James C. McReynolds, Pierce Butler, and George Sutherland. Van Devanter had been appointed by President Taft, McReynolds by President Wilson, and Butler and Sutherland by Harding. The liberal group on the Supreme Court consisted, in 1937, of Benjamin N. Cardozo, Louis D. Brandeis, and Harlan F. Stone, appointed by Presidents Hoover, Wilson, and Coolidge, respectively. In four years Roosevelt had not had an opportunity to fill a single vacancy on the Court. This was the Court that had been invalidating New Deal legislation, with one or both of the duo of Hughes and Roberts usually siding with the conservatives to produce a majority.

For a short time longer, until February 5, Roosevelt kept quiet. He neither said nor did anything about the Court. That day he sent to Congress a message which proposed to reorganize the Federal judiciary. Court dockets, the message said, were overcrowded. More personnel was needed and some of the trouble resulted from "aged or infirm judges." Roosevelt proposed that when a Federal judge who had served at least ten years waited more than six months after his seventieth birthday to resign, the President be allowed to add a new judge to the bench. He could appoint as many as six new Supreme Court justices. The President ran into trouble at once. Even some of his firm supporters thought the means he was choosing to fight a battle that needed fighting was a bit underhanded and oblique. After all, one of his regular supporters on the Court was eighty-year-old Justice Brandeis. His fellow Democrats in Congress had not been consulted at all in advance. Many people felt that the Supreme Court of the United States deserved better treatment than this.

For once everything went against the jaunty President. In March the Court, to everyone's surprise, upheld a Washington minimum wage law much like the New York one it had so recently thrown out. Next month it found the National Labor Relations Act constitutional. In May Justice Van Devanter was prevailed upon to resign, giving Roosevelt a chance to appoint a liberal to the Court. Chief Justice Hughes presented facts that effectively refuted the President's contention that the Court was behind in its work. Before the end of May the unemployment insurance provisions of the Social Security Act had been approved.

Roosevelt still refused to compromise. Then, in mid-July, Democratic Senator Joseph T. Robinson, who had reluctantly led the fight for what opponents called "the court-packing bill" and who had been expected to be Roosevelt's first appointee to the Court, died suddenly. The fight was over. The President named Senator Hugo Black to the bench but suffered further embarrassment, before the Senate confirmed the appointment, when it was revealed that Black had once held membership in the Ku Klux Klan.

Roosevelt later claimed that he had lost the battle but won the war. The Court did shift its viewpoint, largely because within two and a half years Roosevelt was able to name four more justices. The new Court accepted a great deal more national regulation of the economy than had the old. As had been said before, the Supreme Court eventually followed the election returns. Nevertheless, in many respects it was a costly fight for the President and the New Deal. For once, he did not have his way with Congress; he alienated many who had previously been favorably inclined to the New Deal; he strengthened the anti-New Dealers in their opposition. All in all, it was the worst mistake Roosevelt made.

Disaster struck the New Deal on another front in August, 1937. Until then the story of the Roosevelt administration had been one of slow but fairly steady economic recovery. Suddenly there were signs of a recession—a term coined to indicate a slump in business that wasn't as bad as a full depression. The stock market dropped alarmingly; such stocks as General Motors and U.S. Steel fell in a manner only too reminiscent of 1929. The index of industrial production stood at 117 but by May, 1938, it was down to 76. Two-thirds of all the gains of the New Deal years were wiped out. Between Labor Day and the end of the year 2,000,000 lost their jobs.

Roosevelt had bragged that recovery had come because of his program and policies. Now businessmen and Republicans threw the words back at him. Like Hoover before him, if he wished to claim credit for prosperity, then he must take the blame for hard times, too. His opponents, of course, blamed the recession on the policies of the administration. It is more likely that the recession came about because certain New Deal policies had been abandoned. In June Roosevelt, who still in the back of his mind was just as traditionally addicted to the virtues of a balanced budget as Hoover had been, had cut relief spending. Federal Reserve System policies at the same time tended to restrict credit, while social security taxes were beginning to take spending money out of paychecks.

Roosevelt hesitated, beset as he was by one group of advisers which urged caution and economy and another which urged immediate large-scale spending to stimulate business recovery. By April, 1938, the President realized that neither politically nor economically could he wait any longer. He asked Congress for $3,000,000,000 for various forms of relief and public works and Congress voted him that sum plus another three-quarters of a billion. By midsummer, 1938, the recession was ending and recovery continued—aided no little, as time went on, by armament orders from Europe.

The world was moving toward another world war, and internal troubles in several lands did nothing to help the cause of peace. In March, 1936, Hitler had sent German troops into the Rhineland, which had been demilitarized after World War I, and dared anyone, especially France and Great Britain, to do anything about it. No one did. In Russia, meanwhile, a vicious and suspicious Stalin was instituting a reign of terror to purge the land of all opposition to his one-man rule. The purges had begun in 1934 but reached their climax between 1936 and 1938. In 1936 Stalin got rid of a number of old Bolsheviks who had made the mistake of siding with Leon

Trotsky in his losing struggle for power with Stalin. In 1937 Marshal Michael N. Tukhachevsky and other top-ranking officers of the Red Army were tried on charges of high treason and shot. Many elaborate trials were staged in public, at which the accused seemed strangely eager to confess crimes they probably had not committed.

In July, 1936, civil war broke out in Spain, which had been a republic for only five years. A "popular front" government composed of the leftist factions was unable to keep order. The army, encouraged by the Catholic Church and the middle class, revolted, with General Francisco Franco as leader. Like all civil wars the Spanish Civil War was fought with brutality and bitterness on both sides. It also turned into a testing ground for Russian communism and German and Italian fascisim. Soviet Russia assisted the Loyalist government, but at its usual price of trying to take control. Hitler and Mussolini sent troops and equipment to help the Spanish rebels, whose leadership was strongly inclined toward the Fascist system.

Eventually, in April, 1939, the rebels won and the Spanish republican government collapsed. Many persons felt that the Western democracies should have assisted the legitimate government instead of adopting a hands-off policy. Roosevelt took an even more isolationist stand than some of those who had proposed American neutrality legislation. He treated the two sides as though they were each a sovereign state and got Congress to add to the neutrality laws an embargo on the shipment of military goods to countries where there were civil wars. The President thought, along with the leaders of France and England, that a policy of nonintervention in Spain would prevent the civil war from becoming an international one. The cause of the Spanish Loyalists was taken up in the United States with great fervor by many liberals and intellectuals and especially by college students. To them the forces of good and evil were engaged and one could not sit idly by. To many Catholics the rebels seemed in the right. Before the war was over, about 3,000 young Americans fought in Spain on the Loyalist side, mostly with the Abraham Lincoln Battalion, and a number lost their lives. Ernest Hemingway's best-selling novel of the war, *For Whom the Bell Tolls* (1940), has an American hero.

In the fall of 1936 Germany had concluded a treaty with Italy and another with Japan, the latter aimed ostensibly at the international Communist movement but containing secret provisions for military cooperation against Soviet Russia. The three leading Fascist-type governments which were striving the most to revise, by force if necessary, the settlements made at the end of World War I, were thereby united in the Rome-Berlin-Tokyo Axis.

The Japanese militarists were in control of their government and in July, 1937, they struck again in China. Using a clash between Chinese and Japanese troops at the Marco Polo Bridge near Peking as an excuse, they proceeded to bring more of China under their control. As usual, protests citing treaty violations did not cause the Japanese to halt.

Roosevelt, although he had seemed to invoke the neutrality laws more vigorously than necessary, was not an isolationist. On the contrary, he would have preferred to take a fairly firm stand in international affairs but feared to because of the strength of isolationist sentiment among the people of the United States. By the fall of 1937 he felt compelled to speak out in stronger terms than heretofore. In Chicago, the very heart of isolationist sentiment, he delivered what was immediately termed his "quarantine speech," because in it he used the analogy of a quarantine for medical purposes to express what he thought the peace-loving nations should do about aggression. However, he made no specific proposals. Reaction was strong. He was loudly denounced as a warmonger and a few isolationist congressmen foolishly spoke of impeaching him. On the other hand, he received strong support, as evidenced by the letters that came to the White House. For some reason, though, the

President drew back from amplifying or implementing this first step. He refused to admit that quarantining an aggressor meant the same thing as invoking sanctions, that is, embargoing supplies to such a nation.

A test of how the nation felt came soon and brought 1937 to an end on a note ominous for the future. In December Japanese planes bombed and sank a United States Navy gunboat, the *Panay,* at anchor in the Yangtze River in China. Two crew members were killed and eleven injured. Japanese claims of an accident were preposterous. Action would have to be taken, but the nation drew a deep breath of relief when, just before Christmas, the Japanese apologized and offered to pay indemnity. The next month a Gallup poll showed that 70 per cent of the voters favored our complete withdrawal from China rather than run any danger of war.

One international event of 1936 was considered sadly romantic by millions of people around the world. In January, when King George V of Great Britain died, he had been succeeded by his eldest son, the debonair Prince of Wales, as Edward VIII. Edward was still a bachelor at forty-one but had an American friend, Mrs. Wallis Simpson, whom he wished to marry. She, however, was a commoner, and not only had she already been divorced, but she also was now married a second time. Edward wanted to do his duty as England's monarch, but he also wanted to marry Mrs. Simpson even if she could not be queen. This was contrary to all that the ruling classes and the Conservative party of England stood for. Prime Minister Stanley Baldwin told the new King that he could not have both his throne and Mrs. Simpson; and Edward, even though he was supported by romantically minded Winston Churchill, finally had to choose. He picked love over the crown. In December he abdicated, to be succeeded by his brother, the Duke of York, as George VI. In a farewell address, which Churchill may have helped him write and which was heard by radio by millions in the United States and elsewhere, Edward brought many a tear when he concluded:

> I have found it impossible to carry the heavy burden of responsibility and to discharge my duties as king as I should wish to do, without the help and support of the woman I love. . . . And now we all have a new king. I wish him and you, his people, happiness and prosperity, with all my heart. God bless you all! God save the King!

The Duke of Windsor, as he became, and Mrs. Simpson were wed in June, 1937, after her divorce.

The 1930's saw the hopeful rise and the tragic decline of the lighter-than-air ship of the skies known as the dirigible. As early as October, 1930, the British dirigible, the *R101,* on a flight to India, crashed and burned in France with the loss of nearly everyone aboard. The United States Navy thought highly of the rigid airships in those days for patrolling the seas, but the *Akron,* after less than two years of operation, went down in a storm off the New Jersey coast in 1933 with the loss of 73 men. Only three survived. In 1935 the *Macon* broke up off the California coast. The Germans were having better luck and their newest dirigible, the *Hindenburg,* began regular flights in 1936. On one of these, in May, 1937, it sailed majestically over New York in bright sunlight, then headed for Lakehurst, New Jersey, to tie up to the mooring mast. Just as it did so, its hydrogen-filled insides exploded. Thirty-six people died. An account of the landing was being broadcast by radio, so thousands heard the announcer almost break down as the catastrophe took place in his sight.

In the movies in 1936, Charlie Chaplin, still avoiding the talkies, made *Modern Times,* an expression of distaste and dismay as far as twentieth-century technology was concerned. More romantically, Leslie Howard played Romeo in *Romeo and Juliet.* In his comedy hit, *Mr. Deeds Goes to Town,* Gary Cooper gave the world the word "pixillated," and Humphrey Bogart made his first screen appearance in *The Petrified Forest.* The next year was a great one for comedy; not only was there a new Marx Brothers' epic, *A Day at the Races,* there was also a new type of "screwball" comedy, best done by Irene Dunne in *The Awful Truth* and Carole Lombard in *Nothing Sacred.* Pearl Buck's *The Good Earth* was a magnificent film; people enjoyed the movie *Lost Horizon* as much as they had James Hilton's novel; Robert Montgomery was psychopathically menacing in *Night Must Fall.*

In December, 1937, the National Broadcasting Company brought to radio the most famous conductor of the day, Arturo Toscanini, leading an orchestra especially recruited for him. The studio audience was given programs printed on satin so they wouldn't crackle. That same year America lost its great native musical talent, George Gershwin, not yet forty. His most substantial work, the folk opera *Porgy and Bess,* had had its debut in 1935.

In 1936 the playwright Eugene O'Neill became the second American to win the Nobel Prize in literature. In reading matter, the year offered such diverse fare as Dale Carnegie's *How to Win Friends and Influence People* and Van Wyck Brooks's *The Flowering of New England.* In 1937 there was J. P. Marquand's first serious success (and Pulitzer Prize winner), *The Late George Apley,* along with Kenneth Roberts' stirring historical novel *Northwest Passage* and John Steinbeck's tragic *Of Mice and Men.*

In the 1930's a number of new magazines were started. Some succeeded; some didn't last long. On the whole, though, it is remarkable, considering the depression, that so many new magazines were started and made good. Henry Luce, who had been one of the founders of *Time* in the 1920's, was planning a plush magazine to "reflect Industrial Life" just as the stock market crashed. He went ahead, and the first issue of *Fortune,* priced at an unheard-of $1.00 a copy, appeared in February, 1930. Within six years it had 139,000 subscribers and nearly $2,000,000 in advertising revenue. Very much different in content, much more spectacular while it lasted, but a skyrocket that soon descended was *Ballyhoo.* It was first issued in 1931, shot up to a record newsstand sale of 2,000,000 copies, and by its second birthday was falling just as rapidly. It gave a raucous "boo" to all the respectable attitudes and burlesqued the familiar things of life, especially advertising.

Esquire, which when it began publication in October, 1933, was a combination of today's *Playboy* and the men's clothing advertisements in *The New York Times Magazine,* succeeded quickly, partly by publishing the slightly inferior work of top-ranking writers. On the distaff side, in February, 1935, *Mademoiselle* was introduced to young ladies up to the age of thirty and also found a substantial audience. The magazine that set a wholly new style, though, was *Life,* also a Henry Luce production, which made its appearance in November, 1936. It was the first of the modern picture magazines and was tremendously successful from the very start. There were many would-be imitators, but only *Look,* established in January, 1937, and much more sober editorially than the others, has had a lasting success. *Life* reinforced the growing emphasis of the time on photographs in both newspapers and magazines.

Joe DiMaggio joined the New York Yankees baseball team in 1936 and as a star center fielder helped raise to new heights the Yankee dynasty. They won both the American League pennant and the World Series for four consecutive years, beginning in 1936. In 1937 Joe Louis, the "Brown Bomber," born in 1914, the same year as DiMaggio, won the world's professional heavyweight boxing championship by knocking out James J. Braddock. Louis had made boxing a top attraction again, drawing the first million-dollar gate since 1927, when he had knocked out Max Baer in 1935. The next year Max Schmeling of Germany beat him in the only fight he had lost up to then, but he had revenge in 1938 when he battered Schmeling flat in the first round.

Some thought that the sufferings of the depression would cause people to seek comfort and meaning in religion. This did not turn out to be true, except in an area where modern psychology (or the popular idea of it) and religion came together. Henry C. Link's *The Return to Religion* (1936) was a best seller but Link, himself a psychologist, seemed to be saying only that religion correlated with an outgoing personality. At this same time the National Preaching Mission of 1935–36, activated by some of the leading denominations and looking for those troubled by the times, was a failure. In 1937 the Reverend Norman Vincent Peale founded the Religio-Psychiatric Clinic in New York, formally bringing together the newest in mind and soul cures. In 1938 Frank Buchman, an ordained clergyman, opened a campaign known as Moral Re-Armament. The work was carried on through groups gathered informally—in house parties rather than conferences—and featured confessions made in the presence of the group. The most spectacular cult of the period was that of a Negro evangelist, Father Divine, whose real name was George Baker. With his chant, "Peace, it's wonderful," and his "Heavens," he attracted a large following, especially among women. The "Heavens" were establishments where his followers led a group life and they fulfilled the very practical function of providing food and shelter in hard times.

Among the millions of events of 1936 and 1937, we might note four as examples of the variety of life. In 1937 Cristobal Balenciaga opened his Paris fashion salon. That same year Thomas E. Dewey, on his way to becoming governor of New York State and twice losing the race for the presidency, became district attorney of Manhattan. In the summer of 1936 an automatic cotton picker, developed since 1927 by the Rust brothers, John Daniel and Mack Donald, had its first large-scale test. It could pick as much cotton in one hour as eight to ten hand-pickers could in twelve hours. In 1936 Harvard University, the oldest institution of higher learning in the United States, celebrated its three hundredth anniversary with convocations and conferences that spoke up for freedom of inquiry at a time when authoritarian controls were rapidly being clamped on a good part of the world. The occasion reminded the world that leadership in the democratic pursuit of knowledge was passing from the Old World to the New.

8 *Farewell to Reform*

FOR ALL PRACTICAL PURPOSES, 1938 was the last year of the New Deal. After that the congressional opposition to the administration's domestic policies and the deterioration of international relations combined to push aside any thoughts of more reform. Early in 1938 Roosevelt suffered a sharp defeat at the hands of Congress that revealed how greatly things had changed since the honeymoon of the New Deal only five years earlier.

For some time there had been demands from various quarters—including businessmen and President Hoover—that the President's executive office be reorganized to improve efficiency and to meet the demands a greatly changed world placed on the White House staff. Roosevelt's plan, devised by political scientists and public administrators, was first proposed in early 1937 but not acted on. It called for expanding the President's staff, extending the civil service system to many more jobs, putting various independent agencies under one or another of the larger departments, and creating two new cabinet departments, Social Welfare and Public Works. (The Department of Health, Education and Welfare, it might be noted, eventually came into existence in 1953 under the administration of a Republican president.) When Congress finally began to consider the bill in February, 1938, there was a tremendous uproar all over the country. Republicans, conservatives, businessmen, and extremists such as Father Coughlin termed it the "dictator bill." Remembering his defeat over the Supreme Court bill, Roosevelt this time tried to placate his opponents by his reasonableness and to use his political artistry to get the bill through Congress. It was all to no avail. The bitterness of the 1937 Supreme Court fight still lingered and Congress refused to pass the bill.

That same spring Congress did accept a Roosevelt suggestion when it established the Temporary National Economic Committee. Made up of members of Congress and personnel from several Federal agencies, under the chairmanship of Senator Joseph C. O'Mahoney of Wyoming, the committee was instructed to investigate the concentration of economic power in twentieth-century America. The philosophy behind the committee could be traced to the Sherman Anti-Trust Act of 1890, the Clayton Anti-Trust Act of 1914, and the policies of President Woodrow Wilson. In effect, this philosophy said that bigness in business and industry was bad and that it was better to try to break up huge industrial combines into smaller, competitive units than to attempt to regulate the larger, possibly more efficient units. In 1938 the formation of the TNEC also indicated that, for the time being, at least, Roosevelt's advisers who belonged to the old progressive school of thought had triumphed over those who would have business and government cooperate formally, as in the NRA. The TNEC inquiry lasted for three years and the 552 witnesses produced 31 volumes of testimony. The hearings provided a forum for the business community as well as for those suspicious of the motives and actions of industry. While much useful information about modern economic life was assembled, no particular action resulted from the work of the TNEC.

Along with the new Agricultural Adjustment Act already described, the Fair Labor Standards Act, which became law late in June, was the last important reform and recovery legislation of the New Deal. Passed after much opposition from businessmen from the South, where wage rates were lower than in the North, and even from some leaders of the AFL, the law for the first time set a national minimum hourly rate for wages and maximum hours that could be worked without overtime being paid. To start with, the law set 25 cents an hour as the minimum wage and this was to go up to 40 cents in two years. The maximum work week was 44 hours to start with and was to come down to 40 hours in two years. Of course the law applied only to those in industries involving interstate commerce and even then there were many exceptions. In spite of the low minimum and other restrictions, about 750,000 workers got raises as soon as the law went into effect. In addition, the act once and for all forbade the use of child labor (anyone under sixteen) in producing goods in interstate commerce.

Another governmental action of 1938, the results of which are still felt today, was the establishment of the House Committee on Un-American Activities, with Martin Dies, a Texas Democrat, as first chairman. From the start the HUAC was much more interested in pursuing headlines and pet phobias than in doing anything useful or practical. It never defined what an "un-American activity" was. Its main effort was to attempt to find Communist conspiracies everywhere. It seldom did anything about fascism or the extreme right. When it was starting fresh in 1938 it allowed witnesses to make almost any charge without supporting it. In the first few days more than 600 organizations were called communistic. One witness was sure the Boy Scouts and the Camp Fire Girls were dangerous subversive organizations.

Roosevelt met still another setback in the 1938 congressional elections. By mid-1938 he was almost as nettled by the opposition of conservative Democrats, mostly from the South, as he was by that of the Republicans. Finally speaking out as the national leader of the Democratic party—not as President, he was careful to emphasize—he called for the defeat in the primary elections of a number of Democratic members of Congress. The chief of these were Senator Walter

George of Georgia, Senator "Cotton Ed" Smith of South Carolina, Senator Millard Tydings of Maryland, and Representative John O'Connor of New York. Among candidates he did endorse for re-election was Congressman Lyndon B. Johnson. The President's attack on fellow Democrats was quickly labeled the "purge," with its implication of Fascist and Communist methods, by the anti-New Deal forces. In the end, Roosevelt lost all the important primary fights except that against O'Connor, who was defeated. In the November election, the Democratic party lost seats in the House and Senate for the first time in five elections. The Republicans captured 74 more House seats and 7 in the Senate, plus a net gain of 13 governorships. Even so, the Democrats retained control of both houses of Congress.

As the recession ebbed, as political difficulties at home made further reform measures almost impossible, and as the international situation worsened, Roosevelt turned more of his attention to Europe and the Far East. In January, 1938, he asked Congress to increase appropriations for the Navy so that a two-ocean fleet capable of defending both the Atlantic and the Pacific coasts could be built. Many isolationists voted for the bill. Even while it was being debated, Adolf Hitler, after bullying the Austrian government until a new premier invited the Germans in, seized Austria on March 14 and announced "Anschluss," union of that small land with the Third Reich. Other nations protested but took no action.

Hitler next called for self-determination for the allegedly mistreated Sudeten German minority in Czechoslovakia, and by mid-September the world was on the brink of war. France, which had a treaty with Czechoslovakia guaranteeing the latter's independence, wavered; Britain did not want war over "a far-off country of which we know little," as Prime Minister Neville Chamberlain put it; and

Russia, which also had an alliance with the Czechs, did nothing to help. Three times Chamberlain flew to Germany to negotiate with Hitler, who kept increasing his demands. Finally, at the very end of the month, a conference of Hitler, Chamberlain, Mussolini, and the French premier, Edouard Daladier, yielded to Hitler and advised the Czechs to cede the Sudeten area and allow the Germans to enter it. In a short time Poland and Hungary got in on the deal and seized pieces of Czech territory.

Chamberlain flew back to England and proclaimed that the agreement meant "peace in our time." He and his French counterpart were welcomed by their countrymen with cheers for having prevented war. Roosevelt seemed relieved. He had fired off messages to all the leading statesmen involved and had proposed a conference, but the Europeans, believing correctly that the United States was too strongly isolationist to give any military support if France and Britain stood up to Hitler, did not take him or the nation's standing in world affairs very seriously. And so war was postponed but not prevented. The smaller nations of Europe lost faith in the democracies and decided they might as well make the best terms they could with the Nazi regime. Soviet Russia, not invited to the peace meeting, stood more aloof than ever, warily watching both sides. Munich, where the final conference that knuckled under to Hitler was held, and "appeasement," as the policy of France and Britain was labeled, later came to be synonymous with cowardice and the attempt to make a deal with international blackmailers.

Warnings of more danger ahead by Winston Churchill, among others, came true only too soon. In March, 1939, Hitler cynically seized the rest of Czechoslovakia on the excuse of putting down disorders, which his agents had encouraged by pitting the Slovaks against other nationalities. The next month, not to be outdone by his senior partner in aggression, Benito Mussolini and his Italian army invaded and soon conquered tiny Albania.

Meanwhile, on the other side of the world, the Japanese were continuing to extend their control of China, capturing Shanghai, the largest city and greatest seaport, and proclaiming the "Greater East Asia Co-Prosperity Sphere." In July the United States notified Japan it was terminating the commercial treaty of 1911, which was a step toward economic warfare with the Japanese. At this time, rather oddly, some of those who were most opposed to the United States getting involved in any way in Europe denounced the President for not taking more action in the Far East, such as an embargo on trade with Japan.

After Hitler showed by his acts that he would not keep his word, the British and French realized that they would have to take a stand somewhere. Prime Minister Chamberlain, an honest if mistaken man, felt he had been deliberately deceived by Hitler and set out to halt further aggression. Britain and France offered a guarantee of the independence of Poland, Rumania, and Greece. In the summer of 1939 both Germany on the one hand and Britain and France on the other were bidding for the support of Soviet Russia. The Western nations were suspicious of the intentions of the Russians, and the Western leaders did not have much to offer Russia in a tangible way. They also underestimated the strength of the Red Army. Hitler, on the other hand, merely wanted the Soviets to remain neutral when he attacked Poland. He was even willing to let the Russians take some of Poland's territory and do as they wanted with the three tiny Baltic nations.

On August 24, 1939, the announcement that a Nazi-Soviet treaty had been signed spread consternation in most of the rest of the world, especially among the Western negotiators who still thought they had a chance of winning Stalin to their side. War was not far behind. On September 1 the German army invaded Poland. On September 3 Great Britain declared war on Germany, and France unenthusiastically followed suit. World War II had started. By the end of September Poland was crushed by the German blitzkrieg and the Nazis and the Soviets divided up the country. Before the end of 1939, the Russians—safe, so they thought, from Germany—took the occasion to demand territory from neighboring Finland. When the demands were refused, the Russians invaded but for a while were repulsed by their small adversary whose army was adept at fighting in the brutal northern winter. By March, 1940, though, superior Russian power prevailed and Finland had to give up.

As soon as World War II began, Roosevelt went on the radio, presenting in one of his fireside talks the position of the United States as he saw it. He emphasized that he was going to issue a proclamation of neutrality "in accordance with American policy" as well as to meet the requirements of the Neutrality Act. The tone of the speech was sober, its content general; but near the end the President hinted at how he felt:

> This nation will remain a neutral nation, but I cannot ask that every American remain neutral in thought as well. Even a neutral has a right to take account of facts. Even a neutral cannot be asked to close his mind or close his conscience.

The President called a special session of Congress and asked it to repeal the arms embargo in the Neutrality Act. At once all the old arguments and hatreds came out. Much bitterness toward England was revealed. The cry went up again that Roosevelt wanted to be dictator and lead the country into war. The President found it best to stay in the background. It took six weeks for Congress to act. The amended law allowed warring nations to buy arms and munitions but they had to pay cash and had to transport the goods in their own vessels. This was popularly known as the "cash-and-carry" provision. American citizens could not sail on ships of belligerents nor could American ships sail to the ports of warring nations. The Allies had control of the seas and at the start had the necessary cash, so they could benefit by the "cash-and-carry" clause. On the other hand, Hitler was aided in his attempt to blockade England by the part of the law that, in effect, took all American ships off the important parts of the ocean.

Even nature got in its blows in 1938. On September 21, in the midst of the Munich crisis, a tropical hurricane that had come farther north than anyone expected such storms to, struck the northeastern United States, especially New England. More than 600 persons were killed, mostly in the New England states, but some on Long Island. New York City was hard hit; Providence, Rhode Island, had a tidal wave; and all over the area thousands of trees were down, streets were flooded, houses blown over, and communications blacked out. In later years better weather forecasting and the realization that tropical hurricanes could travel north held down the damage and the toll of lives when these storms struck.

For a brief while in the spring and summer of 1939, there were pleasant events to distract the attention of Americans from the war threats in Europe. In June the British monarch, King George VI, and Queen Elizabeth paid a visit to America, the first time a ruling British king had done so. They attracted much attention and presented a favorable picture of often criticized Britain, especially when they enjoyed an American-style picnic at President Roosevelt's Hudson River home at Hyde Park, complete with hot dogs, baked beans, and strawberry shortcake.

The King and Queen were among the millions who visited the New York World's Fair of 1939–40. Under the direction of Robert Moses, who headed a similar enterprise a quarter of a century later, the fair had as its theme "The World of Tomorrow." One of its major areas, where twenty-two foreign nations had pavilions (not including Nazi Germany but including Japan and Russia), was hopefully named "The Court of Peace." There was something for everyone and many new technological marvels, such as television, were demonstrated. For the first time fluorescent lighting was used on a large scale. The most popular attraction was the General Motors Futurama, which purported to show what the world would be like in 1960, especially its cities and highways. By the time 1960 came, the Futurama's predictions had been borne out—only more so.

Thomas Wolfe, burning himself out like a meteor, died in 1938 before reaching his thirty-eighth birthday. In the last of his four autobiographical novels, *You Can't Go Home Again,* which was published posthumously in 1940, he wrote:

> I believe that we are lost here in America, but I believe we shall be found. . . . I think the true discovery of America is before us. I think the true fulfillment of our spirit, of our people, of our mighty and immortal land, is yet to come. I think the true discovery of our own democracy is still before us. And I think that all these things are certain as the morning, as inevitable as noon.

Pearl Buck in 1938 became the third American to win the Nobel Prize in literature. Two new and popular plays written in that year were *Our Town* by Thornton Wilder and *Abe Lincoln in Illinois* by Robert Sherwood. In 1939 America's unofficial poet laureate, Robert Frost, who was already sixty-five but who had many years of writing ahead of him, brought out the second edition of his *Collected Poems.* From another poet, Carl Sandburg, came a volume of his prose biography of Lincoln, *Abraham Lincoln: The War Years.* Three years earlier, in England, there had appeared the first of the Penguin Books, the new-style paperbacks. In 1939 the first of America's modern paperbound books, Pocket Books, made their appearance. Book clubs, too, were gaining. By the late 1930's each of the leading clubs, the Book-of-the-Month Club and the Literary Guild, had several hundred thousand members.

In spite of the threats of war 1939 was a year of comedy hits on the Broadway stage. Clarence Day's humorous and nostalgic portrait of *Life with Father,* published in book form in 1935, was made into a play that ran for seven years after it opened in November. George S. Kaufman and Moss Hart, whose comedy of fey people, *You Can't Take It with You,* had won the Pulitzer Prize in 1936, were now represented by a more biting piece of comedy, *The Man Who Came to Dinner,* the central character of which could not possibly be anyone other than the critic, wit, and raconteur Alexander Woollcott. Finally, there was *Arsenic and Old Lace,* which said that nice old ladies in Brooklyn weren't necessarily as nice as they seemed, but they meant well.

The movies were continuing to entertain America to the extent of 85,000,000 people a week, and $25 a year on the average from each family. For the most part, if one judged life in America by the movies, there was no depression, few troubles of any kind, and the hardest problem of a nation of well-to-do people was to have a good time. In 1932 Hollywood had produced *I Am a Fugitive from a Chain Gang,* while *Our Daily Bread,* in 1934, dealt with subsistence farming. In 1936 there was *Fury,* a realistic film (except for the ending) about lynching, and 1937 brought to the screen a sad story of old age without social security, *Make Way for Tomorrow.* These were the exceptions. In 1938 the most popular movie was easily Walt Disney's first full-length cartoon, *Snow White,* with its catchy songs, especially "Whistle While You Work." In 1939 came *Stagecoach,* which made a star of John Wayne; Laurence Olivier played Heathcliff in *Wuthering Heights;* and Leslie Howard starred in the British film *Pygmalion* about two decades before it reappeared as *My Fair Lady.*

Radio's new hit program of 1938 was "Information Please," urbanely presided over by author and critic Clifton Fadiman and featuring John Kieran and Franklin P. Adams as the regular panelists. It was one of the first of the quiz programs but done with a spirit of fun lacking in later shows. In the fall of 1938 Orson Welles, then only twenty-three, achieved nationwide fame overnight when he scared the country half to death with a radio adaptation of H. G. Wells's science fiction novel *The War of the Worlds.* By changing the time to the present and the locale to New York and New Jersey, he had thousands of listeners (none of whom apparently had ever read Wells's book) believing that monsters from Mars had invaded the Earth that Sunday evening.

For sports fans the saddest event of 1939 was the retirement of Yankee first baseman Lou Gehrig because of illness. Still only thirty-six, he had played for the Yankees since 1925 and had set a record that stands by playing in 2,130 consecutive games. Yet here was the "Iron Horse" struck down by disease. At a farewell ceremony in Yankee Stadium, he gallantly told the packed stands that he was "the luckiest man on the face of the earth" for having had his career. Two years later he was dead of a rare type of paralysis.

Harry James left Benny Goodman's dance band with his trumpet and founded his own orchestra in 1939. That same year he hired as vocalist a young man named Frank Sinatra. That year, too, Skeezix Wallet of the "Gasoline Alley" comic strip graduated from high school. Now he has a son in college. The year before, inventor and aviator Howard Hughes flew around the world in just over ninety-one hours. And in 1938 Tom Mooney was finally freed after providing liberals and radicals with one of their leading causes for many years. Mooney had been sentenced to death, almost certainly unjustly, for the bomb killings in a San Francisco Preparedness Day parade in 1916. His sentence was commuted to life, but many persons never gave up trying to get him pardoned. No protest meeting of the thirties, whether against war or slums or low relief payments, was complete without a few banners reading "Free Tom Mooney."

Nylon began to be produced in quantity in 1939 and soon was

replacing the silkworm as the source of women's stockings. More fundamental work in science was also being carried on in 1939. German scientists demonstrated that the atom could be split. Soon scientists in other countries were pondering over the significance of this discovery, realizing already the enormous energy that could be released if the process could be controlled. In August, 1939, Albert Einstein wrote a letter to President Roosevelt outlining briefly the possibilities now open for producing a bomb of almost unimaginable power. Two months later Roosevelt received another report on the rapid developments in nuclear fission. It likely seemed all very theoretical to the President at first, but once he decided action was called for, he quickly made the first modest plans from which grew the huge Manhattan project and which in less than six years (and a few months after his death) resulted in the first atom bomb falling on Hiroshima.

9 *The Legacy of the Lean Years*

AND SO THE 1930's ENDED and the calendar was turned to 1940, the start of a new decade. Franklin D. Roosevelt was still President, and before the year was out he would be elected to an unprecedented third term; but the New Deal was over. Not so the depression, for as John Kenneth Galbraith wrote in *American Capitalism:*

> The Great Depression of the thirties never came to an end. It merely disappeared in the great mobilization of the forties. For a whole generation it became the normal aspect of peacetime life in the United States—the thing to be both feared and expected. Measured by its continuing imprint on actions and attitudes, the depression clearly stands with the Civil War as one of the two most important events in American history since the Revolution. For the great majority of Americans World War II, by contrast, was an almost casual and pleasant experience.

The events of the spring of 1940 convinced the President and many other Americans that the country must speed up its defense preparations. By the end of June Hitler had overrun Denmark, Norway, the Netherlands, Belgium, and France, and had sent a brave but badly defeated British army fleeing from the Dunkirk beaches back to the British Isles. By September Congress had voted the first peacetime conscription law in the history of the United States. National defense costs had been $633,000,000 in 1933; by 1940 they were $1,457,000,000 and going up fast.

The increased pace of production of implements of war was beginning to further reduce unemployment. The New Deal had cut down greatly the number of men and women out of jobs but the figure was still higher than it had been in 1929 before the crash. Unemployment, in a population of 131,670,000, was down to 7,476,000 in 1940, and total employment was up to 46,468,000, a gain of about 9,000,000 over the low point of 1933. Nevertheless, nearly 14 per cent of the civilian labor force remained out of work.

The Federal government continued to spend more than it was taking in but now the deficit was largely attributable to the armament program rather than relief. During the 1930's the Federal debt increased from about $16,000,000,000 to over $40,000,000,000. In the early thirties, when Hoover was President, the deficits were caused chiefly by declining receipts from taxes; under Roosevelt they resulted more from a deliberate increase in spending. As economic conditions improved and as the New Deal's tax laws went into effect, income from taxes went up. It was $2,700,000,000 in 1931 and $5,900,000,000 seven years later. Deficits were growing bigger too. The President predicted that for the year ending June 30, 1941, it would be more than $13,000,000,000. The notable difference was that neither businessmen nor congressmen, who had professed such alarm over deficit spending for the relief of jobless, hungry people, seemed to worry at all when the money was being spent to arm the country. The result, as far as stimulating business and employment, was about the same.

Nevertheless, business and industry remained solidly aligned against the New Deal, the President, and all their works. Business had been traditionally Republican since the Civil War and the New Deal era reinforced the feeling. The crash and the depression had tumbled business from its pedestal of national leadership and businessmen naturally resented this. The people had seen that, however imperfect the government had been under Roosevelt and the Democrats, it was that government and not business that had done something to bring the nation out of the worst of the depression.

In the process, the Federal government had grown in size and this, too, worried the conservatives. About the time Hoover left office there were 583,000 government employees; by 1939 the number had increased to 920,000. Furthermore, Roosevelt's way of running the government outraged the practical men of affairs (the same ones who, it has been noted, opposed the President when he wanted to reorganize his office in the interests of efficiency). Many of them honestly believed that Roosevelt was trying to become a dictator. It was, in the final analysis, the President's personality that mattered. Samuel Eliot Morison and Henry Steele Commager summed up this aspect of the man in *The Growth of the American Republic:*

> He liked to play his assistants off against each other; he had a pawky sense of humor; he was by turns confiding and secretive, generous and vindictive, clear cut and deliberately fuzzy. Yet in a larger sense he was wonderfully effective: he got things done. He made Washington so exciting that first-rate men left good jobs and came to work for him, and he inspired them with such loyalty that they worked far beyond the ordinary call of duty. Superficially less efficient than President Hoover, Roosevelt was in fact far more effective, and his presidency dramatized once again the vital principle that politics is neither a business nor a science, but an art.

The intellectuals that Roosevelt and the New Deal attracted were both an asset and a liability. Their enthusiasm, their expert knowledge, and, not least, their willingness to experiment were necessary because both political and business leadership was locked in the past. Yet it was only natural for the newcomers to be resented by those who previously had had things their own way. Not a few of the brain trusters seemed so glib, so sure of themselves, that they unintentionally made enemies. Rexford Guy Tugwell was, perhaps, the outstanding example. He had a hard time convincing rural congressmen that he had been born on a farm. Unfortunately for the intellectuals in government, such vocal Communists or near-Communists—fellow travelers—as there were, appeared to be concentrated in the intellectual class. "The New Deal," Richard Hofstadter wrote in *Anti-Intellectualism in American Life,* "brought the force of mind into closer relation with power than it had been within the memory of any living man—closer than it had been since the days of the Founding Fathers." But, he also notes, the feeling against such people that was built up in the 1930's burst out after World War II.

The attitude of youth toward the New Deal and the times in general was somewhat contradictory. By the middle years of the 1930's about 25 per cent of those in their late teens and early twenties had never had a job and a third of all those out of work were in these lower age groups. When employment picked up, the older workers who had held the jobs and who had the skills were rehired ahead of the young men who had never had a job. It was natural that many young people seemed most of all to want security. They didn't expect much, but they were not going to do anything to rock the leaky boat. On the other hand it was possible to point to a small number of young men and women, mostly college students, who were noisily agitating for one cause or another. In the 1930's, apart from arguments about how to cure the depression, the chief preoccupation was the danger of fascism. Mixed with anti-fascism was a strong general anti-war spirit. As a result it was not uncommon to find the participants in a parade or a protest meeting demanding, illogically, both aid for the Spanish Loyalists and an end to war.

When an administration can be summed up under some such label as New Deal, it is natural to try to find in it a philosophy that explains why it did what it did. On examination, though, the New Deal does not lend itself to this kind of analysis. It and its leader were likely to act first and to find a theory to fit later rather than to start with a theoretical system and carry out acts that fitted it. If there had been a theoretical system, the New Deal would not have done so many contradictory things as it did. At times it practiced economy; at others it deliberately unbalanced the budget. At one time it released business from many anti-trust law restrictions; at another it sought to enforce the anti-trust laws more strictly than ever. Unlike fascism and communism, the New Deal had no rigid ideology.

To the extent that it was based on the past, the New Deal stemmed from the populists, the progressives, and other reformers who first became strong about 1890. One of the leaders was Theodore Roosevelt; the other President who carried on the tradition of reform was Woodrow Wilson. There had been a fairly steady reforming current, regardless of party, until the end of World War I. Then came a period of reaction in which the nation fell behind in its governmental and social arrangements in relation to the growth of industrialization and urbanization. By the 1930's the time was ripe, some think, for another round of regulatory and social welfare legislation quite apart from the depression. However that may be, the depression made it imperative that a good deal be done at once that might better have been done more slowly and more deliberately without the pressure of imminent economic catastrophe.

The New Deal differed in some important respects from its ancestors. In earlier times the reformers had believed that government could achieve economic and social justice by a few regulatory laws. It would act as a referee, standing between conflicting interests to insure fair play but not favoring any side. The New Deal advocated a more positive role for government and sponsored legislation to aid one group at the expense of another. Its predecessors had liked to make moral issues out of everything. The New Deal, starting the nation in the general direction of the welfare state, did so for practical reasons. Whether one thinks the New Deal was right or wrong, its leader and his chief assistants saw themselves as doing in "the American way" what needed to be done in the modern world at a time of crisis. In this view the New Deal was no sharp break with the past but was a period of acceleration, trying to speed up the social machinery to reach the point where it would have been if it had not stalled earlier.

At the start of the period many economists and other experts believed the nation had reached "economic maturity." The rate of population growth was declining; the western frontier was closed and no longer offered an outlet for surplus labor; there seemed to be no new inventions or technological advances on the horizon. These assumptions led to caution and an attempt merely to get the already existing machinery going again. No thought was given to expansion; rather, it might be necessary to curtail production in some areas, such as agriculture. As it turned out, these assumptions were all wrong. In the 1930's the population increased by just under 9,000,000 persons; but in the 1940's, in spite of the war, the increase was 19,000,000; and in the 1950's the gain was nearly 28,000,-000. Stimulated by World War II, invention and discovery gave industry many new products, particularly in the fields of electronics and synthetics.

It was also in the 1930's that a new economic doctrine, replacing Adam Smith's eighteenth-century laissez faire theory, was formulated and began to be accepted. It was just in time to have some effect on the New Deal but too early to be accepted wholeheartedly even by some New Dealers. The new principles were those of John Maynard Keynes, the British economist, whose chief work, *The General Theory of Employment, Interest and Money,* appeared in 1936. He had been advocating his unorthodox ideas earlier and in May, 1934, he and Roosevelt met in the White House. Unfortunately, they seem to have rubbed each other the wrong way. Keynes was a bit the overbearing Englishman who, according to the President, talked like a mathematician. To Keynes, the President seemed hopelessly ignorant of any economic theory. As far as policies to cure a business depression were concerned, Keynes's basic remedy was that the government should spend enough to get business, employment, and investment operating again at a higher and a self-sustaining level. The New Deal followed the Keynesian theory but only part way. It spent, but not enough, and it stopped too soon. This, said the converts to Keynes, was why there had been a recession in 1937–38. The administration spent enough to alarm the business and financial community but not enough to cure the depression. Also, Keynes's call for government intervention to stimulate the economy implied that business had failed.

With its progressive background, contradictory policies, and dabblings in a new and untried economic system, how can the New Deal be summed up? To quote Professors Morison and Commager again:

> In so far as the New Deal was directed toward an extension of government control over national economy, it was in the progressive tradition; in so far as it was directed toward improving the welfare of the common man, it was in the democratic tradition. Taken as a whole, the New Deal legislation contributed greatly to both recovery and reform, improved the status of the farmer and the laborer, prepared the way for a more equitable distribution of wealth, brought business, banking, securities, utilities, and transportation under more effective regulation and, most important of all, helped to salvage the natural resources of the nation. At the same time it interfered with the freedom of business enterprise, inaugurated far-reaching controls over labor and farming, encouraged the growth of bureaucracy, stimulated class antagonisms, greatly increased the national debt, and at some points challenged traditional readings of the Constitution. However the historian may wish to strike the balance between credits and debits, three things are clear: the New Deal, in one form or another, was inevitable; it was directed toward preserving capitalistic economy rather than substituting another system; and the methods employed were in the American tradition.

But whatever the New Deal was as a philosophy of government or as an economic system, it took its particular form from the personality of Franklin Delano Roosevelt. An aristocrat by birth, he genuinely liked people for what they were, else he would not have been so sensationally successful as a politician. Such a man could relish reminding the Daughters of the American Revolution "that all of us, and you and I especially, are descended from immigrants and revolutionists." A cripple largely confined to a wheel chair for more than twenty years, he never let it stop him from doing what he wanted to do—sailing, traveling all over the country time and time again. He was not afraid to lead—which has been an attribute of all our great presidents—and yet he knew that at times the leader could not get too far ahead of his followers lest he lose them. A marvelous political campaigner, he mastered the new techniques needed for effective radio-speaking so well that millions of people felt his fireside chats were "my President speaking to me."

Sometimes he was needlessly devious; sometimes he seemed to be backing conflicting points of view; but most of the time he dominated the government, the politicians, his assistants, Washington, the newspaper headlines. He had courage, spirit, determination. You might not like the way he used these personal traits; you might not be in favor of his program; but you certainly couldn't ignore him. There was no neutral ground: either you hated the man or you loved him. There were many more of the latter than of the former. As was shown by the crowds that cheered him when he lived and mourned him when he died suddenly in 1945 with victory so near, he was the only chief executive between Woodrow Wilson and John Fitzgerald Kennedy who reached the emotions of the people.

The historians and the political scientists are already placing Franklin D. Roosevelt among the nation's great presidents, along with Washington, Jefferson, Jackson, Lincoln, Theodore Roosevelt, and Woodrow Wilson. Samuel Eliot Morison summed up the results of Roosevelt's domestic policies in *The Oxford History of the American People,* writing that his "administration saved twentieth-century

American capitalism by purging it of gross abuses and forcing an accommodation to the larger public interest." And in *The American Mind* Henry Steele Commager thought: "History may record that he did more to advance democracy than any president since Lincoln and as much to strengthen capitalism as any statesman since Hamilton."

The English historian Sir Isaiah Berlin in 1955 recalled that in the 1930's "the only light in the darkness" was Roosevelt and the New Deal. He continued:

> What attracted his followers were countervailing qualities of a rare and inspiring order. He was large-hearted and possessed wide political horizons, imaginative sweep, understanding of the time in which he lived and of the direction of the great new forces at work in the twentieth century—technological, racial, imperialist, anti-imperialist. He was in favor of life and movement, the promotion of the most generous possible fulfillment of the largest possible number of human wishes, and not in favor of caution and retrenchment and sitting still. Above all, he was absolutely fearless.

No one has summed up this sometimes contradictory man better than James MacGregor Burns in *Roosevelt: The Lion and the Fox:*

> To examine closely single aspects of Roosevelt's character—as thinker, as organizer, as manipulator, as strategist—is to see failings and deficiencies closely interwoven with the huge capacities. But to stand back and look at the man as a whole, against the backdrop of his people and his times, is to see the lineaments of greatness—courage, joyousness, responsiveness, vitality, faith, and, above all, concern for his fellow man. A democrat in manner and conviction, he was yet a member of that small aristocracy once described by E. M. Forster—sensitive but not weak, considerate but not fussy, plucky in his power to endure, capable of laughing and of taking a joke. He was the true happy warrior.

Looking back at the 1930's, it is almost impossible to believe that for so long during the depression so little would have been done to end it, to improve business conditions, to take care of jobless people without income. We cannot understand the "villains" of the era, such as Andrew Mellon, who thought there was nothing to do but to let nature take its course. They were unintentional villains. They didn't know any better and they couldn't be made to believe that it was possible for men to put a stop to a depression. It had never been done.

One is just as puzzled as to why thousands, even millions, of ordinary people would take years of depression, hunger, and poverty, without revolting or at least without taking some overt, vigorous action outside the usual channels of politics and business. As we have seen, such physical violence as occurred consisted of scattered incidents. Communism might have been expected to make converts by the hundreds of thousands and yet it was almost completely without influence except for a small number of noisy intellectuals and others, most of whom renounced communism by the end of the decade. The patience and faith of the American people passed all understanding.

Perhaps we are less surprised by, but also less aware of, the effects of the depression that are still today influencing our ways of doing business and of running our government. Several writers have referred to a depression "scar" the nation bears. In March, 1966, John Fischer, in a "Letter to a New Leftist, from a Tired Liberal," wrote in *Harper's Magazine:*

> If you really want to understand the behavior of the middle-aged generation, you must look first at its history. It has been through two major wars and a depression. These were experiences which you cannot even imagine—but I hope you will take my word for it that their impact was heavy and lasting. They shaped the character and outlook on the world of everybody who went under the hammer. If you prefer the word "distorted" rather than "shaped," I won't argue; in any case, they left a lot of scar tissue.

As World War II neared its end, the great fear of businessmen, government officials, and workers was that there would be a depression as soon as the shooting stopped. Almost everyone assumed that a depression was inevitable. As it turned out, everyone was wrong, largely because some positive steps were taken to ease the transition from a wartime economy to a peacetime one. The most significant sign of all was the passage of the Employment Act of 1946, which declared that it was now the policy of the United States government to assure high employment and production. Without specifying any means, the Federal government, carrying out what undoubtedly were the wishes of the citizens, said it would never allow a depression to occur again if it could possibly help it. Out of the depression and World War II there came some good. The depression made it certain that in the future government, business, and economics would not sit idly by as they did at the start of the Great Depression. World War II stimulated science and technology to such an extent that the problems of business and economics were altogether changed in the postwar years compared with the 1930's and 1940's. Finally, as far as the lasting influence of the depression is concerned, one must take into account the fact that more than a quarter of the present population of the United States remembers the depression years, or some of them. This in turn means that many of the men and women in top positions of authority in government and business carry that "scar," the recollection that there is such a thing as a Great Depression and that it is a terrible, frightening thing.

We are now far enough away from the 1930's to feel nostalgic about the decade, even those who suffered. Some of the styles of the period are being revived. The Rainbow Room restaurant on the sixty-fifth floor of the RCA Building in Rockefeller Center has reopened, bragging that it looks as it did in the thirties when it was new. It was a period no one who lived in it will ever forget; but no one would want to live it over again.

Reading List

In the following list the publisher and the date of publication are those of the original edition. If that edition is paperbound, it is so indicated. A number of the other titles are available in paperbound editions as well as in the editions listed here.

Allen, Frederick Lewis. *Since Yesterday.* New York: Harper & Bros., 1940.

Bird, Caroline. *The Invisible Scar.* New York: David McKay Co., Inc., 1966.

Burns, James MacGregor. *Roosevelt: The Lion and the Fox.* New York: Harcourt, Brace & World, Inc., 1956.

Chambers, Clarke A. (ed.). *The New Deal at Home and Abroad, 1929–1945.* New York: Free Press, Macmillan Co., 1965. Paper.

Daniels, Jonathan. *The Time Between the Wars; Armistice to Pearl Harbor.* Garden City: Doubleday & Co., Inc., 1966.

Galbraith, John Kenneth. *The Great Crash, 1929.* Boston: Houghton Mifflin Co., 1955.

Keller, Morton (ed.). *The New Deal: What Was It?* New York: Holt, Rinehart and Winston, 1963. Paper.

Leuchtenburg, William E. *The Perils of Prosperity, 1914–32.* Chicago: University of Chicago Press, 1958.

———. *Franklin D. Roosevelt and the New Deal, 1932–1940.* New York: Harper & Row, Publishers, 1963.

MITCHELL, BROADUS. *Depression Decade; From New Era through New Deal, 1929–1941.* New York: Holt, Rinehart and Winston, 1947.

NEW YORKER, THE. *The New Yorker Twenty-Fifth Anniversary Album, 1925–1950.* New York: Harper & Bros., 1951.

RAUCH, BASIL. *The History of the New Deal, 1933–1938.* New York: Creative Age Press, 1944.

——— (ed.). *The Roosevelt Reader: Selected Speeches, Messages, Press Conferences, and Letters of Franklin D. Roosevelt.* New York: Holt, Rinehart and Winston, 1957. Paper.

ROGERS, AGNES (ed.). *I Remember Distinctly; A Family Album of the American People 1918–1941.* New York: Harper & Bros., 1947.

ROOSEVELT, ELEANOR. *This I Remember.* New York: Harper & Bros., 1949.

SCHLESINGER, ARTHUR M., JR. *The Age of Roosevelt.* Vol. I: *The Crisis of the Old Order, 1919–1933.* Vol II: *The Coming of the New Deal.* Vol. III: *The Politics of Upheaval.* Boston: Houghton Mifflin Co., 1957, 1958, 1960.

SHANNON, DAVID A. (ed.). *The Great Depression.* Englewood Cliffs: Prentice-Hall, Inc., 1960. Paper.

STEINBECK, JOHN. *The Grapes of Wrath.* New York: Viking Press, 1939.

SWADOS, HARVEY (ed.). *The American Writer and the Great Depression.* Indianapolis: Bobbs-Merrill Co., Inc., 1966.

TAYLOR, DEEMS. *A Pictorial History of the Movies.* New York: Simon and Schuster, Inc., 1943.

WECTER, DIXON. *The Age of the Great Depression, 1929–1941.* New York: Macmillan Co., 1948.

Acknowledgments

The brief quotations in this book are from the following sources:

ALLEN, FREDERICK LEWIS. *Since Yesterday*. New York: Harper & Bros., 1940.

BURNS, JAMES MACGREGOR. *Roosevelt: The Lion and the Fox*. New York: Harcourt, Brace & World, Inc., 1956.

COMMAGER, HENRY STEELE. *The American Mind*. New Haven: Yale University Press, 1950.

GALBRAITH, JOHN KENNETH. *American Capitalism: The Concept of Countervailing Power*. Boston: Houghton Mifflin Co., 1952.

HOFSTADTER, RICHARD. *Anti-Intellectualism in American Life*. New York: Vintage Books, Random House, Inc., 1966.

KELLER, MORTON (ed.). *The New Deal: What Was It?* New York: Holt, Rinehart and Winston, 1963.

MORISON, SAMUEL ELIOT. *The Oxford History of the American People*. New York: Oxford University Press, 1965.

MORISON, SAMUEL ELIOT, and HENRY STEELE COMMAGER. *The Growth of the American Republic*, Vol. II. New York: Oxford University Press, 5th ed. 1962.

RAUCH, BASIL (ed.). *The Roosevelt Reader: Selected Speeches, Messages, Press Conferences, and Letters of Franklin D. Roosevelt*. New York: Holt, Rinehart and Winston, 1957.

SCHLESINGER, ARTHUR M., JR. *The Age of Roosevelt*. Vol. II: *The Coming of the New Deal*. Boston: Houghton Mifflin Co., 1958.

STEINBECK, JOHN. *The Grapes of Wrath.* New York: Viking Press, 1939.

WILSON, EDMUND. *The American Earthquake.* New York: Anchor Books, Doubleday & Co., Inc., 1964.

WOLFE, THOMAS. *You Can't Go Home Again.* New York: Harper & Bros., 1940.

Harper's Magazine. March, 1966.

The New York *Sunday News.* August 7, 1966.

The New York Times. October 30, 1929.

Saturday Review. May 21, 1966.

Index